AF411937

the London café book 2.

AUTHOR
SIMON GARNER

PHOTOGRAPHER
GILES STOKOE

PUBLISHED BY
SALAMANDER BOOKS LIMITED
LONDON

a **salamander** book

8 Blenheim Court, Brewery Road
London N7 9NT
United Kingdom

© Salamander Books Ltd 2001

A member of the Chrysalis Group plc

ISBN 1 84065 242 X

Commissioning Editor
Charlotte Davies
Editorial and Design
Joanna Smith
Reproduction
Studio Technology

Based on an original concept by
Helen Stone
Original design concept
Graham Mitchener

10 9 8 7 6 5 4 3 2 1

Printed and bound in Italy

Acknowledgments
We would like to thank all the café owners, chefs and staff who took the time to help us. Thanks go to all the people who kindly gave their permission for us to reproduce their words and images.

Contents

London has changed a lot since the first London Café Book appeared three years ago.

We have a new millennium, a new Tate gallery, a mayor, new phone numbers and a giant Ferris wheel. Shoreditch is full of bars, Clerkenwell is following suit, Notting Hill is full of film crews, Southwark is the place to be and Clapham is reverting to its natural state as a suburb of Surrey.

Everyone is drinking coffee. On every high street Starbucks, Costa Coffee, The Seattle Coffee Company, Café Nero and Aroma squabble over vacant real estate; but this book isn't really about coffee. It is about cafés. It is a celebration of the places themselves and of the diversity of London's café culture; from the quirkiest caff to the luxury of a hotel tea.

In making our selection we have tried to stick by the principles of the first London Café Book.

Each featured café should have something special about it: it might be the decor, the location, the food, the atmosphere, the owner, the clientele or even just the concept. All of the twenty-two cafés included in this volume are new to the London Café Book, many of them because they have only opened their doors in the last three years, some of them because they are classics that we missed the first time round.

Since this is the second book, it seems appropriate to make some observations on the changes that have occurred in the capital's cafés over the last three years. One of the first things of note is the steady progress of the organic movement. No less than three of the cafés featured in this book are fully organic, and many of the others make use of organic produce when they can. No doubt, as awareness increases, many more organic establishments will be opening up. A far less health-conscious trend that has also become apparent is the resurgence of the English cooked breakfast. The traditional fry-up is no longer the exclusive preserve of the greasy spoon caff. Londoners, it seems, are turning away from the croissant, and particularly at weekends a late cooked breakfast has become part of the social calendar – especially for those who have indulged themselves a little too much the night before. Over a third of the cafés featured in this book offer a special all-day breakfast menu at weekends.

Juices, too, are now well established in London's cafés. Many places now sell smoothies and vegetable juices. Several of the cafés in this book will make them up from scratch and one of them is a dedicated juice bar, though, of course, it still serves coffee and cake. Likewise, computer terminals are far more common than they used to be, even in cafés that do not regard themselves as Internet cafés. But for all these apparent changes, the essence of what makes a good café remains the same.

What is essential is atmosphere.

It can be grand or humble but it must be different from what you would find in the office, at home or on the street: because above all a café is a kind of refuge from normality, it is a place to take a break from everyday life.

And if there is one thing that we have discovered in the course of making this book it is that running a café is a demanding and labour-intensive job. Our **thanks** go out to all the café owners, managers and staff who took the time to talk to us and made our job so much easier than it could have been.

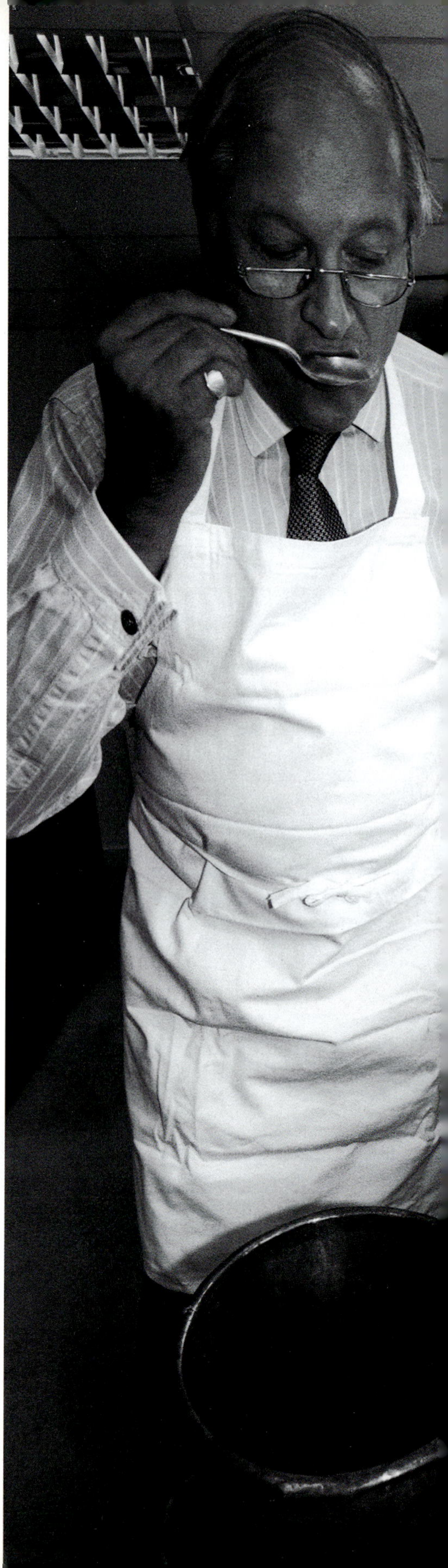

"The thing about tea is that a whole lot can go wrong between picking the green leaves and putting it in the packet. We are looking to pick up faults in manufacture that might detract from the value of the tea, and also to spot any seasonal variations, because the quality of the leaf can vary from one week to the next and even from one part of the estate to another. Some people liken it to wine tasting – it is not quite as exotic, but it is a similar sort of process." Mike Bunston, Director

Wilson Smithett

202 Blackfriars Road
London SE1 8NJ

It may not be readily apparent
from the number of coffee shops
on the high street, but Britain is still
a country of tea drinkers. Measured
by volume, tea outsells coffee 2:1.
We import 140 million kilos of tea
a year and on average we consume
about three and a half cups of tea
per head per day. Tea is
undoubtedly the national response
to any crisis, and recent research
has also indicated that it is a
healthy drink that helps to break
down cholesterol in the blood.
These days the vast majority of tea
is sold in its country of origin and
the London Tea Auction closed
down two years ago. However, on
Blackfriars Road, at Wilson Smithett,
one of London's few remaining tea
brokers, samples of tea are still
tasted every day.

For the purposes of tasting, the tea is made very **strong** – 5.6 grams is brewed for 6 minutes before being poured out into the cup where, except in the case of very delicate teas, **milk** is added. The liquor is then tasted and careful observations are made of both the **dry** and the **infused** leaf.

'You are looking for a reasonable degree of **colour** and strength, a reasonable degree of **brightness**, and a reasonable degree of **briskness** – that is the liveliness on the palate. The more of those things you've got, the better the **quality**. Mike Bunston'

"Tea all comes from the one leaf, the **Camellia sinensis**. And truly anything that is called tea should come from *Camellia sinensis*. Today people talk about **herbal** teas, but they have got no connection with tea whatsoever. One of the few things I like about the **French** is that they call them by the proper name: they call them tisane or **infusions**, which is what they are." Mike Bunston

"I still think that on a **blazing** hot Saturday afternoon when you have been working in the **garden** a nice hot cup of tea is the most **refreshing** drink you can have." Mike Bunston

"There is no secret to making tea. The problem with most people today is that they throw a teabag in a mug and expect it to infuse in seconds. You are never going to make a good cup of tea that way. You need to treat it with respect and obey the three basic rules: good ingredients, fresh boiling water, and a decent time to brew." Mike Bunston

'I can't think of anything worse than waking up in the morning and drinking a cup of coffee. I've got to have at least two cups of tea to get me going. Mike Bunston'

Frances and Abdel Boukraa originally met in Paris. They then lived in Tunisia for five years where they ran a small hotel and restaurant before returning to London in 1989. In London they were surprised to find that there was nowhere to get good North African food.

Adams Café

77 Askew Road
London W12 9AH

On a bleak stretch of Askew Road, between Shepherd's Bush and Acton, Adams Café can easily be mistaken for your average greasy spoon. However, this intriguing and friendly café is, in fact, a schizophrenic affair. In the mornings it serves up tea, sausages and bacon to local builders, and only a band of North African tiles around the walls hints at its double life. In the evenings, however, Adams Café transforms itself into an excellent Tunisian and Moroccan restaurant, serving couscous and tagines to customers from all over London.

When they came back to London in 1989 the prices were sky high and Abdel and Frances couldn't afford to buy into a restaurant property anywhere in London, so they decided on a café instead.

'The couple we bought the café from really helped us. After they had sold it to us they stayed with us for two weeks helping us to learn the ropes and get to know the customers, and how to make a really good cup of tea and good bacon and eggs.

Frances Boukraa, Proprietor

"The thing about **working** in a **café** is that your job is to make people **happy**. I wouldn't want to be a parking attendant where your job is to make people's lives a **misery**."

Frances Boukraa

"You get people who come in here **every single day** and order exactly the **same thing**. So by the time you see them crossing the road you have already poured out their cup of tea and their **order** has gone through to the **kitchen**." Frances Boukraa

salade Tunisienne

serves 4

salad

1 green pepper, cored, deseeded and
  finely chopped
3 tomatoes, cored and finely chopped
½ cucumber, finely chopped
½ onion, finely chopped
1 apple, cored and finely chopped
a few mint leaves, chopped, or
  1 teaspoon dried mint
juice of ½ lemon
3 tablespoons olive oil
salt and pepper

+

shredded lettuce
tinned tuna, drained and flaked
2 hard-boiled eggs, sliced
a few black olives
crusty bread to serve

Mix the chopped pepper, tomato, cucumber, onion and apple in a large mixing bowl. Add the mint, lemon juice, oil, and salt and pepper to taste and mix well. Arrange the shredded lettuce on a large serving plate and spoon the salad on top. Garnish with a little tuna, the egg slices and a few black olives. Serve the salad with crusty bread.

"After we had been here for a year we went to the bank and asked for a loan. We told the manager that we wanted to be a restaurant at night. He said: 'Oh yes, what is your speciality?' So we told him it was couscous, and he said: 'What's that?' I explained that it was a sort of semolina. That did it. We didn't get the loan." Frances Boukraa

"All the **changes** we have made came about very **gradually**. You have got to be very careful with a café not to alter it too radically or you lose your **clientele**. The people who come into cafés every day like the **familiar** surroundings, they don't like to see change."
Frances Boukraa

In the **evening** you get people who have got a little more **money** to spend – the **chattering classes** of Shepherd's Bush, I suppose. Frances Boukraa

"We do a selection of **Moroccan wines**. And we have some Tunisian wine too, but it is difficult to get and we have to import it through **Paris**, so we can't keep it on the wine list. We've also got some **Tunisian spirits**: Thibarine which is a **date liqueur** and Boukka which is made from **figs**."
Abdel Boukraa, Proprietor

Lamb Tagine with Fresh Mint   serves 4

Tagine

1kg (2lb 4oz) boneless lamb, cubed

1 onion, sliced

2 garlic cloves, crushed

1 teaspoon dried mint

1 tablespoon paprika

2 tablespoons tomato purée

2 tablespoons olive oil

1 teaspoon saffron

1 sprig of rosemary

2 bay leaves

1 sprig of thyme

4 tomatoes, quartered

2 green peppers, sliced

4 potatoes, quartered

2 sprigs of mint

salt and pepper

boiled rice to serve

Garnish

finely chopped onion

finely chopped flat-leaf parsley

Preheat the oven to 180C (350F/gas mark 4). Place the lamb, onion, garlic, dried mint, paprika, tomato purée, olive oil, saffron, rosemary, bay leaves and thyme in a large casserole dish. Add water to just cover the ingredients, place the lid on the casserole and cook in the preheated oven for 1 hour.

Add the tomatoes, peppers and potatoes to the casserole, stir to mix, then cook for a further hour until the meat is tender and the vegetables are cooked through, removing the lid after about half an hour to reduce the sauce to a rich consistency. Add the fresh mint for the last 5 minutes of cooking time and season to taste. Sprinkle the casserole with finely chopped onion and parsley and serve with boiled rice.

6 I still do some of the **preparation** *for the evening.*
The secret to Tunisian cooking is in the **spices**
The main thing is a lot of spice: chilli sauce, tomato sauce, coriander, cumin and chilli.
Abdel Boukraa *9*

'The inspiration for the name is a surrealist poem by a guy called Eluard, written in the 1920s. It is about the earth being blue like an orange, and it is completely off the wall – and I just thought it was really nice. It was very instant.'

Daren Bonar, Proprietor

The Blue Orange

65 Columbia Road
London E2 7RJ

When, on a Sunday morning, you see someone coming towards you hugging a plant, you know you are getting near to Columbia Road, the home of London's weekly flower market. At the heart of this pretty little East End street, if you can find it behind the foliage, is The Blue Orange, a Moroccan-tinged utopia with garden chairs and orange walls opening out at the rear to a ramshackle old dairy yard. It is the ideal place to pause between horticultural purchases or simply to while away the morning over a coffee and a newspaper.

The Blue Orange started life as a coffee bar above the courtyard to the rear of the present shop. "When we opened down here, we thought it would die upstairs. A lot of people say that they like it down here, but on a Sunday it is too busy. Upstairs is quieter; it is above the bustle of the market and you can hide in a corner and read your paper." Lee Bonar, Proprietor

Daren Bonar also runs two shops importing furniture from Morocco.

Everything in here is for sale. Well, you can't actually buy the table you are eating off… but I can order one for you. Daren Bonar

"I found these kids in Marrakesh doing it on the wall and decided to do it too — just to say this is my place." Daren Bonar

6 Basically what
we wanted was a nice
atmosphere, nice
decor, good **coffee**, nice
music and that is it. I know what I
would want if I wanted to have a coffee
and **relax** for an hour, so I just
tried to do that. **9**
Daren Bonar

"This **area** has changed a lot. When I
moved here it was **cheap**. Now it is
expensive. The ladies in the
laundrette hate it because their kids can't get flats round here – but then they also think
Lord Mountbatten is Prince Charles' dad." Nigel Barrett, Customer

"There's a lot of
energy in the
East End. I've
got another shop in
Notting Hill but there
is a very different
atmosphere. And
Notting Hill
is supposed to be
really **trendy**, but
it has got much more
soul to it here
really." Daren Bonar

"I came into it totally naïve. I'd never done a cappuccino in my life. But that is the **best way** sometimes. If it doesn't work, at least you can say you've tried it." Lee Bonar

'We hadn't been out for breakfast for almost three years, then we discovered this place, and now

"There are no **customers** here. I think he's just got a big extended **family**." Ian Smith, Customer

Blue Orange Filled Sweet Bread

per serving

1 Portuguese sweet bread or brioche
mayonnaise
mustard
2 slices of smoked ham
grated mature Cheddar cheese
1 vine-ripened tomato, sliced

slice the brioche or sweet bread horizontally and spread with a little mustard and mayonnaise. Fill with ham, grated cheese and sliced tomatoes, and serve.

here **three times** in **three weeks**. Helen Simpson, Customer *9*

"The people who **work** here on Sundays do it because they **like** it – even when they have got a full-time job during the week. Even my **Dad** comes in to help in the morning." **Daren Bonar**

Apple Pie

(recipe from Daren and Lee's mum)   serves 8

225g (8oz) self-raising flour
115g (4oz) butter or margarine
1 egg
680g (1lb 8oz) cooking apples,
   peeled and chopped

a few cloves
1 teaspoon ground cinnamon
honey to taste
1 beaten egg to glaze
brown sugar for sprinkling

Preheat the oven to 200C (400F/gas mark 6). To make the pastry, place the flour in a bowl and rub in the butter or margarine until it forms fine breadcrumbs. Stir in the egg and a little water if necessary to form a soft dough. Roll out the pastry on a floured board and use to line a 12-inch greased pie plate. Trim the edges. Place the apples in a pan and add a few tablespoons of water. Cook over a low heat until slightly softened. Add the cloves, cinnamon and honey to taste, then spoon the apples on to the pastry base. Brush the edges of the pastry with beaten egg. Reroll the pastry trimmings, cut out thin strips and use them to make a criss-cross pattern over the top of the apples. Brush the strips with the remainder of the egg, then sprinkle the pie with brown sugar. Cook in the preheated oven for 20–30 minutes until the pastry is golden.

28

"You sit **outside**, and then you can pop across the road and get some whelks. **Coffee** and **whelks** – it's a great **hangover** cure, I can tell you." Nigel Barrett

Café del Parc

167 Junction Road
London N19 5PZ

It would take quite a feat of the imagination to confuse Tufnell Park with Ibiza, but step inside Café del Parc on Junction Road and it doesn't seem quite so ludicrous. For a start, the music is spot on – a succession of intriguing and chilled-out tunes from the inspiration for the name, Café del Mar. And the decor too is bright, cheery and Mediterranean, though a projector has to replace the famous sunsets. But Café del Parc is not just about atmosphere, it is also about good food. From an open kitchen in the centre of the room, Steve Morrish is centre stage creating culinary delights from an ever-changing menu.

31

*It is like having **dinner** at **home**, like a **party** at home, so you can be what you want to be. The only thing is, it should be much **bigger**.*

Chetna Patel, Customer

Steve and Alan live downstairs. In fact, the café used to be their front room until they converted it into a vegetarian delicatessen in 1991 and finally knocked the walls through to create Café del Parc in 1998.

"The reason why the chairs outside aren't all the same is that they kept getting stolen. Every weekend one more would disappear. They took a table too, but we got that back because I ran after them. It's a lovely area." Alan McNally

"I went to Café del Mar in 1990 and people say it changes your life – well, they did in those days. And it just made me think that there was more to life than what I was doing. I even had the name Café del Parc sorted out before we opened the deli." Steve Morrish

‘The **music** in this place is second only to the **food** – I spend a fortune on **tapes**.’
Steve Morrish

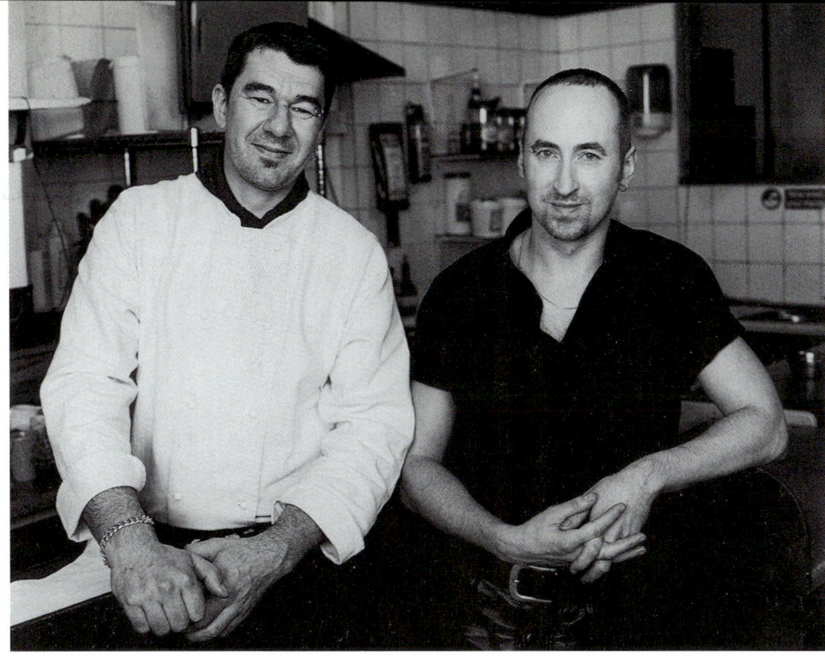

“The first time we tried to come here they had run out of everything. There was a big sign in the window saying: **‘Sorry, no food’**. But we still came back anyway.” Philippe Coley, Customer

“I particularly recommend the **veg breakfast** – they do the greatest **banana fritters** in North London.” Andy Gilbert, Customer

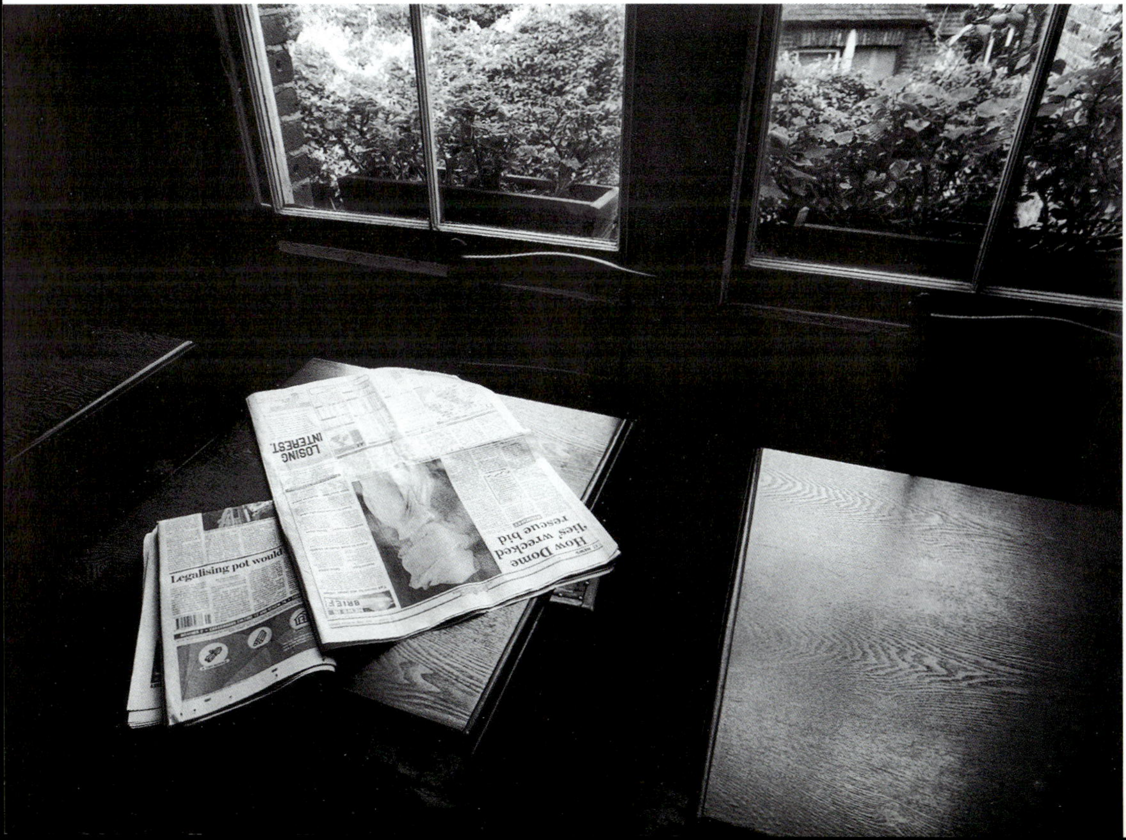

"The **music** is excellent, really **excellent**. It is nice to have something that is **chilled out**, but that you can still get **engrossed** in.
Chetna Patel, Customer"

"Customers are always asking what we are **playing**. They often ask Steve for **compilation tapes**. One day he actually gave a woman a tape and she was so touched she burst into **tears**." Alan McNally

"Never even **dream** of asking to turn the **music down** in front of Steve.
Alan McNally"

Stuffed Meatballs in Tomato and Pesto Sauce   serves 4

450g (1lb) lean minced beef

1 onion, finely chopped

3 garlic cloves, crushed

1 bunch of basil

175g (6oz) Mozzarella

10 sundried tomatoes in oil

oil for frying

flour for coating

2 x 400g (14oz) cans chopped tomatoes

2 tablespoons tomato purée

1 tablespoon pesto

sugar, salt and pepper

black olives, cherry tomatoes, basil, parsley and chives to garnish

350g (12oz) garlic and basil tagliatelle, cooked, or plain tagliatelle, cooked and tossed with
   chopped basil, olive oil and garlic to serve

Preheat the oven to 190C (375F/gas mark 5). Mix the minced beef with half the onion,
half the garlic, 8–12 finely chopped basil leaves and salt and pepper. Finely dice half the
Mozzarella, and chop three or four basil leaves and four sundried tomatoes very finely; mix
these together in a separate bowl. Take a ball of beef mixture, about the size of an apricot,
and flatten with floured hands until it is about 8cm/3in across. Place a teaspoon of the
Mozzarella mixture in the middle and close the beef around it to form a ball. Continue
until all the ingredients are used up.

Heat 2.5cm/1in of oil in a frying pan, roll the meatballs in seasoned flour and fry until
browned on all sides. Remove and place in an ovenproof dish. To make the sauce, sweat the
remaining onion and garlic in a little oil until translucent. Add the tomatoes, tomato
purée, pesto, and sugar, salt and pepper to taste. Pour over the meatballs, cover and cook in
the preheated oven for 40 minutes. Arrange the meatballs on top of the tagliatelle, cover
with the remaining cheese and melt under a grill. Garnish with the remaining sundried
tomatoes, the black olives, cherry tomatoes, basil leaves, chives and chopped parsley.

Chicken Breast Stuffed with Chorizo, Mushrooms and Garlic in Rhône Sauce *serves 2*

2 skinless chicken breast suprêmes

1 small chorizo

6 button mushrooms

2 garlic cloves, crushed

1 small onion, finely chopped

60g (2oz) butter

flour for coating

oil for frying

6 large basil leaves

1 large glass red Rhône

2 teaspoons tomato ketchup

1 teaspoon demerara sugar

salt and pepper

broccoli to serve

Garnish

tomato wedges

basil, parsley and chives

Preheat the oven to 200C (400F/gas mark 6). Remove the small fillet from the back of each chicken breast. Place the breasts on a chopping board, cover with clingfilm and bash with a meat tenderizer or rolling pin until they are the size of an open hand. Next bash the small fillets until flat.

To make the stuffing, finely chop one-third of the chorizo and two of the mushrooms and mix with half the garlic, 1 teaspoon of the onion, the butter and salt and pepper. Place half the stuffing on the centre of each breast and place the fillet back on top. Fold in one long edge, followed by the boneless end, then fold over the other edge and secure firmly in place with cocktail sticks. Roll the breasts in seasoned flour.

Fry the chicken parcels in hot oil until browned on all sides, then add the remaining onion, garlic, the basil and a few slices of chorizo to the pan. Cook until the onion is translucent, then add the wine, ketchup, sugar and seasoning. Finally add the remaining whole mushrooms and half the cream. Transfer to the preheated oven and cook for 25 minutes or until the chicken is cooked through. Place each breast on a plate and make a slit half way along. Place the sliced chorizo in the slit and garnish with the mushrooms, basil leaves, chives, chopped parsley and tomato wedges. Drizzle over the remaining cream and serve with broccoli.

"I just take weird ideas and put them together somehow. I like to try and do unusual things, but I have to really enjoy what I am cooking. I like to experiment. Generally I suppose an idea will just come to me, but you never know whether it is going to sell or not. Like putting a Parmesan crust round deep-fried Brie and serving it with mango – but that is going really well." Steve Morrish

My secrets are coming out now. I use ketchup in some of the sauces. Steve Morrish

"It's ersatz Vienna with Hampsteadian overtones. Though, of course, nothing can ever replace the real Viennese coffee houses, where you could sit for hours with one cup of coffee and they would bring you endless glasses of water while you read all the newspapers." Dr Antscherl, Customer

Café Mozart

17 Swains Lane
London N6 6QX

Café Mozart has recently celebrated
its tenth birthday, but when you sit
inside, surrounded by the wood-
panelled walls and the hissing of
the espresso machine, it is easy to
believe that it has been here
forever. It is classically continental,
a little piece of Vienna transported
to the edge of Hampstead Heath;
the perfect environment in which to
enjoy an extensive menu ranging
from English breakfasts to goulash,
schnitzel and a variety of salads –
but make sure you leave room for
one of Café Mozart's fabulous
home-baked cakes with schlagobers
(fresh whipped cream).

"My father is **Viennese** and a lot of his family live in London. We keep the **standard** high because if the **Sachertorte** wasn't up to scratch, they would be very quick to let me know. They are not the most **forgiving** of families."
Vanessa Schon,
Proprietor

"My friends used to say that the people here are posh and **tease** me for working in a **posh place**. But the customers are nice people and **well mannered**. It is very intimate here, everyone knows each other and is very **friendly**."
Luana Munteanu,
Waitress

Its proximity to **Hampstead Heath** makes Café Mozart a popular stopping off place for parents, **dog-walkers** and **joggers**. Outdoor heaters and an awning ensure that the **pavement tables** are habitable at virtually any time of year.

'You get some customers who come in and always have the **same thing**, so we know them not just by name, but by their orders. We order by the name of the customer; there is one guy who always comes in and has a milky cappuccino, and his name is Billy, so we just say, **'one times Billy'**, and everyone knows what it is. And a 'one times Sybil' is a cappuccino, croissant and marmalade. **Theresa Cunniffe**, Manager'

Beef Goulash serves 4

4 onions, roughly chopped
1 garlic clove, crushed
1 tablespoon vegetable oil
2 teaspoons caraway seeds
1 beef stock cube
2 teaspoons Hungarian paprika
900g (2lb) lean stewing beef, cubed
400g (14oz) can chopped tomatoes
1½ red peppers, roughly chopped
½ green pepper, roughly chopped
900g (2 lb) potatoes, cubed

Sauté the onions and garlic in the oil until translucent. Add the caraway seeds, stock cube and the paprika and stir well. Next add the meat and sauté fast until it is lightly browned all over.

Add the tomatoes, cover the pan, reduce the heat and simmer for half an hour. Add the peppers and potatoes, turn the heat down low and cook gently until the vegetables are cooked and the meat is tender, stirring occasionally to prevent it sticking.

'The chefs are really worried out the back. We've put them all in hats. I think they think you are health and safety.'
Vanessa Schon

"The cakes and pastries are very good. My father comes from **Bratislava** – that is only 30 minutes from **Vienna**, just across the border. We come here every Sunday afternoon and he really likes the cakes – he says they are very **genuine**."
Sebastian Rice,
Customer

Chocolate lovers should try one of Café Mozart's famous **hot chocolates**.

It is like half a cup of hot chocolate **mousse**. Some people **love** it and some people **hate** it. It is **very, very rich**. Vanessa Schon, Proprietor

"When we get **new people** in here they sometimes ask: 'What cakes do you do?' Well, where do you start? You have to narrow it down a bit and say: 'Do you like **Gâteaux**? Do you like chocolate?' And if they can't decide what they want, I always recommend the baked **cheesecake** or the Maronentorte."
Theresa Cunniffe

Maronentorte serves 10

Cake

5 eggs, separated
300g (10½oz) caster sugar
225g (8oz) unsweetened chestnut purée
125g (4½oz) dark chocolate, melted

Cream

450ml (¾ pint) whipping cream
150g (5½oz) dark chocolate, melted and cooled
3 egg yolks
2 teaspoons instant coffee granules, dissolved in 1 tablespoon boiling water

To make the cream, whisk the whipping cream until it forms stiff peaks. Mix the chocolate with the egg yolks and coffee, then fold in the cream. Chill in the refrigerator for 24 hours.

Preheat the oven to 180C (350F/gas mark 4). To make the cake, beat the egg yolks and sugar together until light and fluffy, in an electric blender if you have one. Add the chestnut purée and melted chocolate and mix well. Whisk the egg whites and 2 tablespoons of caster sugar until they form stiff peaks. Fold them gently but thoroughly into the chocolate mixture.

Divide the mixture between two 9-inch greased and floured baking tins. Bake in the preheated oven for 35–40 minutes until just cooked through. Test with a skewer to check it is cooked: insert the skewer into the centre of the cake and if it comes out clean the cake is cooked. Turn out of the tins and cool on a wire rack.

When the cake has cooled, sandwich one-third of the cream between the two cake layers and then cover the cake with an even layer of the cream mixture. Refrigerate until ready to serve.

If you can handle the pronunciation, why not try some
Sommer Welschriesling Trockenbeerenauslese
– an Austrian dessert wine from the shores of the Neusiedlersee.

"It is really really Austrian and it is very good wine and it is only in the top places – the guy who sold it to me said he'd only been able to sell it to places like the Savoy – and I went for it just because I think it is so good. It is not cheap, and it may not work, but I'll drink it and not worry. On a cold day I can't think of anything better than a piece of cake and a glass of dessert wine." Vanessa Schon

SHII-TAKE
RIS...
MEL
de
MUNTANYA
A.BRATO
FEUDI
DI·SAN
GREGORIO
MINESTRA
CEREALI
SALA CEREALI
Parmalat
Salsa della nonna
Pomodoro
LaSelva
Piccante
"Arrabbiata"
AGLIANICO
DEL VULTURE
1997
D'ANGELO
TONNO
PECORINO
D'ORO
£ 1.75 per 100grm
MASCARPONE
Roquefort
French Blue
1.90 per 100g
VIGN
Triple C

The Deli Bar

117 Charterhouse Street,
London EC1M 6AA

It may only have been here for just over two years, but The Deli Bar is already something of a veteran in the fast-expanding restaurant, club and café scene of Smithfield. Tucked into a side street beside the meat market at the quiet end of Charterhouse Street, the café upstairs provides a stylish setting for breakfast, lunch and morning coffee, while the delicatessen downstairs is an epicure's paradise, catering to the busy lunchtime take-away trade.

> What we try to do is keep things very, very **simple**. What we do is source very **good products** – like our pasta: we fly it in twice a week from this little factory outside Milan.
>
> Mike Foskett, Proprietor

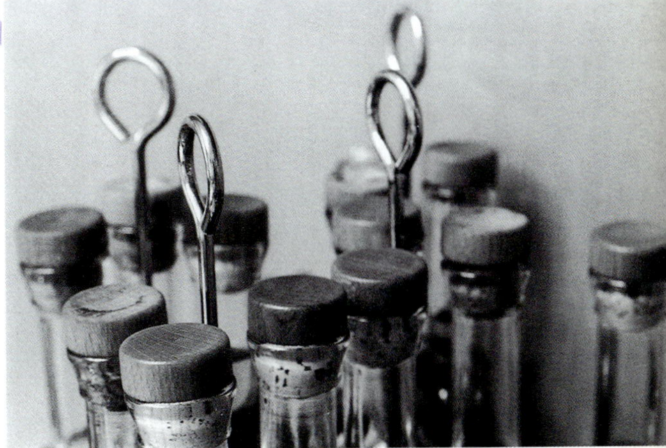

In Smithfield it is not unusual to see people enjoying a pint of **Guinness** with their **breakfast**. Because of the **meat market**, many of the pubs in the area open at six o'clock in the morning.

'I like it because it's **different**. It's not a pub. It has a very different atmosphere to a pub. And the people, they are all **local people**, very **arty** and **diverse**, and the food is lovely. You come in here and you always end up **talking** to someone you've never met before.'

Aida Muro, Customer

Mike used to live in Italy. It was his experience of the combination of food, wine and coffee available in Italian enoteca that inspired him to open The Deli Bar.

"The idea was to combine a delicatessen with a café and a bar. In Italy you don't have Starbucks. In Italy you go into a café-bar and you can have a coffee, you can have a beer, you can have a Spumanti or a glass of wine – I mean, how many coffees do you want to drink a day?" Mike Foskett

"We're very women-friendly here. For some reason we get lots of groups of women in the evening. They know that, apart from me, no one is going to pester them." Mike Foskett

6 Most of the food in the deli comes from Italy. The salami is all from Rome or Napoli or Milan. But some of the cheeses are from France and Spain. 9
Emanuel Lamy, Assistant Manager

"I've been here seven months, but it only seems like yesterday that I was saying that I had only been here a week. I love it here. The staff are all from **different countries** with different ways of life. And we have a lot of regular customers — we get to know them all."
Natasha Poledica, Waitress

"The front section of the building used to be a **salt-beef factory** – if you look at the stairs you can see the **salt** coming through the **paint**. We've coated it with all these special paints but it keeps **coming back**." Mike Foskett

Doing a thing like this you learn your **limitations** – and this is way beyond my limitations. Mike Foskett

Coddled Eggs with Pancetta *per serving*

a knob of butter
2 eggs
a little pancetta (smoked Italian bacon), chopped
salt and pepper
buttered toast to serve

Gently butter the insides of two egg coddlers or poachers and break the eggs into them. Divide the pancetta and remaining butter between them, then season the eggs with salt and pepper.
Cover the pan and cook for about 6 minutes. Turn the eggs out on to hot buttered toast and serve immediately.
As an alternative, the pancetta can be replaced with smoked salmon, a little grated cheese, a few fried mushroom slices or a sprinkling of fresh herbs.

51

The **historic plaques** on the wall in the rear room of The Deli Bar are listed monuments and cannot be removed. They date back to the time when the **poor** of the parish of St Sepulchre used to come here to collect their **alms**.

"Every time anyone has a beer or coffee here, a small portion of the **price** goes to **charity** – well, we pay rent to a charity." Mike Foskett

The Smithfield *per serving*

2 slices of prosciutto di Parma
2 slices of bresaola
2 slices of mortadella
4 slices of salami
2 slices of speck
2 slices of prosciutto cotto alla erbe

4 pieces of sundried
   tomato in oil, drained
olives
olive oil for drizzling
olive bread

Arrange the cured meats artfully on a serving plate. Chop up the pieces of sundried tomato, combine with a handful of fat, juicy olives and scatter over the meats.

Drizzle with a little olive oil, then serve with hunks of olive bread.

The daytime menu at The Deli Bar has a resolutely **Italian** flavour, while in the evenings **tapas** is available.

> Sometimes, if I get **bored** and he's very **busy**, I help the cook. He's **Spanish** too and he's very, very nice. He makes really good **tapas**.
>
> Aida Muro

*I **never** drink coffee. I'm a tea drinker, and I get very **distressed** if it is not done properly. I've been barred from a tea room in Suffolk because I complained about the size of the **teapot**. I said: 'If that is tea for one, I'll have tea for **four** please.' It was a bank holiday Monday and the woman said: 'I've had enough of your sort all weekend,' and **threw** me out.*

Rose Ratcliffe, Proprietor

Grace & Favour

35 North Cross Road
London SE22 9ET

Part shop and part tea room, Grace
& Favour is a serene and dreamy
oasis situated in the quiet side
street that is gradually transforming
itself into the bohemian heart of
East Dulwich. Whether you are
looking for afternoon tea, an
excellent home-cooked lunch or
just browsing for a birthday present,
Grace & Favour provides the perfect
combination of clutter and good
taste to revive the spirits.

> ❝ A cafe needs to have a **personal** touch. It needs to have someone making **decisions**. Someone has to decide that we're not selling Coke or cappuccinos. Too many places are so market researched that they end up being **bland**, they end up being Ford Mondeos. **Steve Laws**, Waiter ❞

During the week, the **menu** changes every day, while at the weekend an all-day **brunch** menu is particularly popular with **locals**.

"We do a whole range of **cordials** and people really like them. The most **popular** is the elderflower." Tracy Foster, Merchandiser

A former art student, Kensington market stallholder and stylist for Elle Decoration, Rose Ratcliffe started Grace & Favour when she took over a former Caribbean food store and motorbike repair shop on Northcross Road in 1997.

"It's completely different from anywhere else I've worked – I don't know why, but it's got an incredibly serene atmosphere. And it doesn't seem particularly contrived – it just is." Steve Laws

6 Customers say that being in here makes them feel restored and ready to face the world again. And I think, how can I make a calm place – I'm completely manic. Rose Ratcliffe 9

Sweet Potato and Brown Lentil Soup *serves 4–6*

3 red onions, finely chopped
3 celery sticks, chopped
3 tablespoons olive oil
115g (4oz) brown lentils
handful of coriander leaves
dash of dark soy sauce
¼ chilli, finely chopped
2 sweet potatoes, chopped
900ml (1½ pints) vegetable stock
400g (14oz) can chopped tomatoes
salt and pepper

Garnish
coriander leaves
crème fraîche
Parmesan shavings

Fry the onions and celery gently in the olive oil for about 10 minutes until soft but not browned. Add the lentils, coriander, soy sauce and chilli and stir well. Then add the sweet potatoes, stock and tomatoes and simmer for 45 minutes on a low heat. Season to taste and blend the soup if you like a smooth consistency. Spoon a little crème fraîche on top of each portion and top with a few coriander leaves and Parmesan shavings.

Grace & Favour prides itself on being child-friendly. Toys are provided and there is plenty of space for buggies as well as books and magazines for the adults.

"I have to hand it to Rose, she is so patient. I've seen her pick up babies to stop them crying, or so that the mother can eat. I run a pub so I deal with drunk people all the time, but I can't handle mothers." Trisha Ledwith, Customer

6 I don't like **signs** everywhere. We don't have a sign saying 'no smoking' and we don't have a sign saying '**toilet** this way' either. I think that if you signpost everything, then no one **talks** to each other. You don't have **signposts** at home saying where the loo is. *9*

Rose Ratcliffe

"You get people in here who say: 'Oh, I've got a wheat **allergy** and I can't eat **dairy**,' and then you come out of the kitchen and see them eating **banoffi** pie." Rose Ratcliffe

Grace & Favour is known for its satisfying **breakfasts**, croissants, delicous **pancakes** and selection of tempting homemade **cakes**.

"People say there's nothing for **children** to eat, but there is plenty for children to eat. What they mean is that we don't do **kiddy** portions of fish fingers and **beans**." Rose Ratcliffe

Chocolate and Orange Soufflé Cake serves 8–10

400g (14oz) good quality dark chocolate
280g (10oz) butter
10 eggs, separated
225g (8oz) caster sugar
4 tablespoons Camp coffee
4 tablespoons cocoa powder
grated zest of 1 large orange

Preheat the oven to 190C (375F/gas mark 5). Grease an 8-inch cake tin
and dust with cocoa powder, shaking out the excess. Melt the chocolate
and the butter in a heatproof bowl over a pan of gently simmering
water. Allow to cool a little, then whisk in the egg yolks, sugar, coffee,
cocoa and orange zest. Whisk the egg whites until they form stiff peaks,
then gently fold into the chocolate mixture, a little at a time, until
well incorporated. Turn the mixture into the prepared tin and bake for
45 minutes until the cake has set right through. Allow to cool in the tin.
Serve with cream or crème fraîche and dust the top of the cake with
cocoa. Cut the cake with a wetted knife as it is very sticky.

"Don't say I'm into **astrology**. People will think I'm a real **flake**." Rose Ratcliffe

It was recommended to me by my hairdresser. You can go into neutral in here, which is just what I want. It is nice just to be in your own space.
Clare Mackie, Customer

The Green

60 New Kings Road
London SW6 4LS

Parson's Green, at the end of the New Kings Road, was originally southwest London's bohemia, but now it is just as upmarket, if a little quieter, than its neighbour Chelsea. And with the green still at its heart it retains something of a village feel. With its sleek, curved, steel-topped counters, Internet access, magazines and newspapers, The Green café pulls in a largely local lunchtime crowd to enjoy a range of good value soups, toasted sandwiches and pasta specials.

63

"We **make** everything here, we have a big **kitchen** downstairs and we do everything **ourselves**. That is why people come back." Charles Green, Proprietor

The **melts** are very popular, and so are the **pasta** dishes. And every day I have to make three or four **specials**. Most of them just come to me when I come in in the **morning**. Del Galliford, Chef

The customers are great – no one complains so they must be alright. **Del Galliford**

"It is really the only **good** place round here to eat that isn't a restaurant. They are so **friendly** and they always treat me – and they do outrageous **smoothies**. You can pick your fruit, but I just always ask Charles to make me up something **good**." Maria Meyers, Customer

65

"It is a **local** area here, we have a lot of **regulars** with the local people. We open at **seven** o'clock and a lot of people come in here for the breakfasts and **lunch** is very busy, but from four o'clock it is **dead**."

Charles Green

Smoked Salmon and Spinach Quiche *serves 8*

<u>Pastry</u>
225g (8oz) plain flour
115g (4oz) butter or margarine
pinch of salt

<u>Filling</u>
4 large eggs
150ml (¼ pint) milk
300ml (½ pint) single cream
pinch of dry mustard
115g (4oz) spinach, wilted
115g (4oz) smoked salmon
salt and pepper

+

a selection of salads to serve

Preheat the oven to 200C (400F/gas mark 6). To make the pastry, place the ingredients in a food processor and process, adding a little water if necessary, to form a soft dough. Roll out the pastry on a floured surface and use to line a 9-inch quiche dish. Chill for 30 minutes, prick the base a few times with a fork and bake in the preheated oven for about 10 minutes, until the pastry is crisp and golden. Remove the pastry case from the oven and lower the oven to 160C (325F/gas mark 3).

Break the eggs into a mixing bowl and add the milk, cream and mustard. Whisk well and season to taste with salt and pepper, then set aside. Arrange the wilted spinach in the bottom of the pastry case and lay the smoked salmon on top. Pour the egg mixture over the spinach and salmon, then return to the oven to bake for about 45 minutes or until the egg mixture is just set. Serve hot or cold with a selection of salads.

I have a **shop** round the corner selling painted **furniture** and I've become a bit of a **regular** in here. I just put a note in the window saying I'll be **back** in 20 minutes. If I'm not in by two o'clock Rosie starts saying: '**Where's Maria?**'

Maria Meyers

"**Business** is getting better and **better** here. There are lots of **nice shops** opening." **Rosie Green**,

Proprietor

"I'm not an **aficionado** of cafés, but I love **staring** at people – I'm a people **watcher**." Clare Mackie

Pasta with Chicken and Sundried Tomatoes in a Tomato and Basil Sauce

serves 4–6

1 large onion, chopped
3 garlic cloves
2 tablespoons olive oil
60g (2oz) flour
600ml (1 pint) chicken stock
60ml (2 fl oz) white wine
2 tablespoons tomato purée
400g (14oz) can peeled plum tomatoes, liquidized
225g (8oz) cooked chicken, shredded
225g (8oz) sundried tomatoes in oil, chopped
a handful of basil leaves
450g (1lb) pasta such as farfalle, freshly cooked
salt and pepper

Fry the onion and garlic in the olive oil until soft, then add the flour and mix well. Add a little of the chicken stock and the white wine, bring to the boil and allow the liquid to reduce a little. Add the tomato purée, plum tomatoes and the remaining chicken stock. Bring to the boil again, reduce the heat and simmer for 30 minutes.
Add the chicken, sundried tomatoes and basil to the sauce and warm through for about 5 minutes. Season to taste and pour over the hot pasta. Mix well, transfer to a serving dish and serve hot.

The Green is famous for its weekend brunch – The Full Monty – a sumptuous breakfast of eggs, bacon, beans, mushrooms, Cumberland sausages, French fries, grilled tomatoes, freshly squeezed orange juice, plus coffee or tea

6 If they don't
get eaten today,
they'll go in the bin.
Charles Green 9

The Hive

Lavender Hill
London SW11 5TN

Battersea Arts Centre is well established as one of London's foremost venues for new and experimental theatre. Housed in the Old Town Hall building on Lavender Hill, it contains two studio theatres, a main house, rehearsal spaces, a gallery and a bar. What is less well known is that it also contains a spacious and relaxed café that offers tea, coffee, snacks and a changing menu of Mediterranean food to the general public as well as to the artists and actors working in the building.

'Initially we were going to call it the Buzz Bar but then we decided on The Hive. We wanted to carry the bee theme through from the mosaic in the foyer. We've even got honey-dripped walls.

André Bell, Proprietor

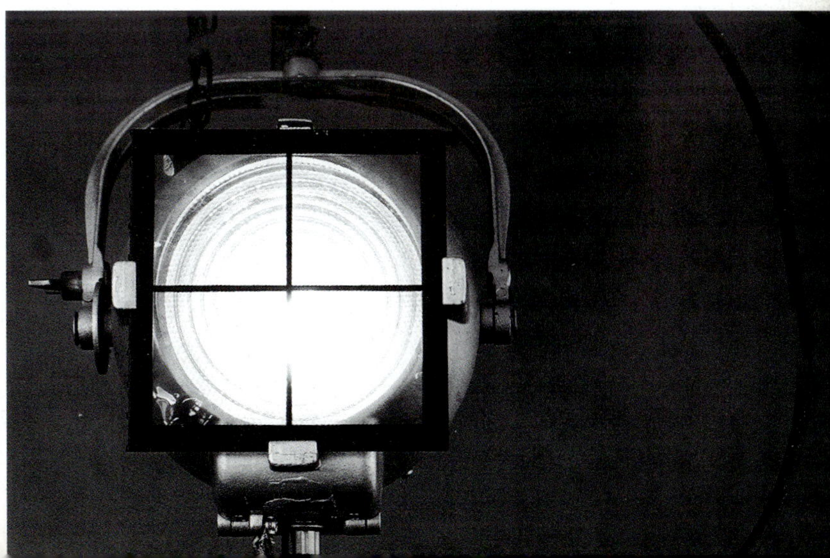

The bee mosaic on the floor is unusual, but it is not unique: the same design is also to be found on the floor of Manchester Town Hall.

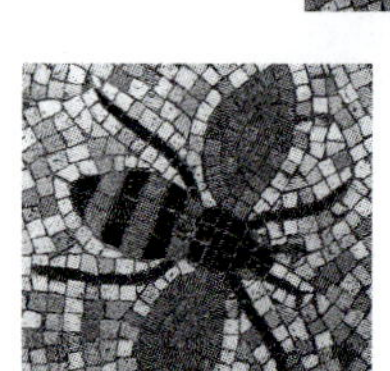

No one seems to know the real reason for the bee mosaic, but there are all sorts of theories: that they are worker bees and they represent industry, that this is Lavender Hill and there used to be hives here, or maybe just that it is B for Battersea.
Emma Hickman, BAC

The small stage in The Hive is used for regular musical and spoken word performances in the evenings.

"I used to be a **barman** not a chef, and I've never been trained as a chef. The **inspiration** comes from my own personal **passion**."
Enrico Addis, Chef and Proprietor

Maybe in **another life** he was a chef – because he told me he had **never** cooked before, but it is so **good**. Celia Mendes, Waitress

"I want it to be **child**-friendly. There aren't many places round here where **mothers** can take their kids. Wednesday at about three o'clock we get the **baby brigade** – sometimes there are 15 pushchairs in here." **André Bell**

Battersea Municipal Buildings and

Town Hall first opened its doors to the public on 15 November 1893. The architect was Edward Mountford who also designed the **Old Bailey** and Battersea Library.

"There is a **sense** of **community** here that I like. Local people come in, and they remember when they used to have **teenage** dances in here. They have lots of fond memories of **kissing** behind the partitions." André Bell

'The **aim** was to do a range of food which is **healthy** and suitable for everyday meals but which, at the same time, is something **interesting**. I'm constantly experimenting, but I always listen to **feedback** from the customers − I think that is very important.'
Enrico Addis

Macarrones de Busa all'Agnello *serves 6*

(Sardinian Pasta with Lamb)

2 tablespoons olive oil
300g (10½oz) minced lamb
4 sundried tomatoes in oil
1 large onion, finely chopped
2 garlic cloves, crushed
1 glass dry white wine
1 tablespoon paprika
vegetable or meat stock
handful of parsley, finely chopped
handful of basil, finely chopped
1 small red chilli, finely chopped
salt and pepper
500g (1lb 2oz) fiorelli or other egg pasta, cooked
100g (3½oz) Pecorino cheese, grated

Heat the oil in a large frying pan, add the lamb, sundried tomatoes, onion and garlic and cook until the lamb is golden. Add the wine and paprika and continue to cook at a gentle simmer. When the pan is almost dry, add a little stock to moisten the mixture and continue cooking and adding more stock as necessary for 30 minutes. Allow the mixture to dry again, then add the herbs and chilli and season with salt and pepper. Toss the cooked pasta with the sauce, then finally add the grated Pecorino cheese and serve hot.

Polpettine di Melanzane serves 4

(aubergine fritters)

2 large aubergines   breadcrumbs
1 large egg   salt and pepper
60g (2oz) Parmesan, grated +
1 garlic clove   olive oil for frying
1 tablespoon chopped mint   humus to serve
2 tablespoons chopped parsley salad leaves to garnish

Cook the whole aubergines for about 20 minutes in a pan of boiling water, then drain. Peel off the skins and squeeze out any excess moisture, then place the flesh in a blender and blend to form a smooth mash. Add all the remaining ingredients, gradually adding more breadcrumbs until the mixture can be rolled into balls.
Fry the balls in olive oil over a gentle heat until lightly browned all over. Serve hot with humus, garnished with salad leaves.

A close examination of the **cherubs** above the grand staircase in the foyer will reveal that one of them has a **pierced nipple**: a minor alteration made by one of the **builders** when the building was renovated in 1992.

"I
like the way that
Leicester Square is always
changing. You just have to
look out of the window and there is
always some **weird** stuff going on. It
keeps me **entertained** – I get
bored really **easily**. Cheryl
Murphy, Waitress**"**

Home Internet Café

1 Leicester Square
London WC2H 7NA

Leicester Square might be a Mecca for tourists, buskers and people who paint themselves silver and stand very still, but until recently it has had little to offer anyone looking to surf the net or relax over a coffee. The opening of the Home Internet Café on the first floor of the Home building has changed all this. Providing 11 terminals, great coffee, juices, smoothies and good, straightforward food in a sleek yet comfortable modern environment, it is a splendid vantage point from which to enjoy a view of the crowds.

When Home opened in late 1999 it was one of London's first **super-clubs**. Occupying the whole of the corner building it includes the Internet Café, several club floors, a restaurant and the administrative offices of the Home organization. Home can be contacted on the web at **www.homecorp.com**.

"Nobody noticed the building. Nobody remembers what it was before. In fact, it was just an office block with an Aberdeen Steak House on the ground floor."
Rhondda Pierre, Manager

'You do get people coming in who don't know anything about computers – and I kind of like it. I like helping people like that, helping them to set up an account and educating them about the Internet – because it is so important.'
Abigail Hills, Waitress

6 Friends sometimes ring me up and say: 'Where are you?' I say: 'At Home.' And they say: 'Oh, I'm just round the corner from you. I'll **pop** in.' So I have to say: 'No, I'm not at home. I'm at work.' Rhondda Pierre **9**

"The most popular thing is the iced coffees. They look really nice. People don't realize what they are, but when they see someone else ordering a glass, they say, 'What's he drinking? I want one the same.' " Alex Olabarri, Waiter

Whardorf salad

per serving

Salad
1 green apple, cored and diced
1 dessertspoon sultanas
1 dessertspoon raisins
2 celery sticks, chopped
8 walnut halves, chopped

Dressing
1 tablespoon mayonnaise
1 tablespoon freshly squeezed orange juice

+

lettuce leaves, tomato wedges and cucumber slices to garnish

To make the dressing, whisk together the mayonnaise and orange juice until smooth. Toss the salad ingredients with 1 tablespoon of the dressing and serve the remainder of the dressing as an accompaniment. Serve the salad in a lettuce-lined bowl, garnished with tomato and cucumber.

Although the Swiss Centre may have moved out of its premises next door, its bells and mechanical figures continue to draw a small crowd at midday.

"The bells can drive you mad. But at least you know what time it is. We used to open at twelve and if the bells started and the door was still closed, I knew I had to get going." Rhondda Pierre

'The **buskers** in Leicester Square must be the most annoying buskers in London. There's a guy out there who plays the **Titanic** song on some sort of oriental violin every night at the same time – you can set your **watch** by him.'
Rhondda Pierre

The curious **pods** above the escalators at the entrance are, in fact, cashiers' booths. They are lowered **hydraulically** to ground level when the club is open in the evenings.

"It is all planned with **military** precision – but somehow, something or other will always manage to go **wrong**."
Rhondda Pierre

Prawn Mary Rose *per serving*

200g (7oz) peeled prawns
2 tablespoons mayonnaise
2 dessertspoons tomato ketchup
2 tablespoons lemon juice
Tabasco sauce
salt and pepper

+

2 small baguettes
butter
sliced cucumber
tomato and lemon slices
to garnish

Mix the prawns, mayonnaise, ketchup and lemon juice in a bowl until well combined. Add a few dashes of Tabasco and season to taste with salt and pepper. Mix again thoroughly. Split the baguettes horizontally, butter lightly and fill with sliced cucumber and prawns. Garnish with cucumber, tomato and lemon slices and serve.

> This is not a **cold** place. It is the kind of place you feel like coming back to. We've had people who were only on **holiday** in London for a week, and they came in here four or five times – by the end of the week they knew all our **names**.
>
> Alex Olabarri

"There is a Home philosophy and it is about connecting with people. For example, around the building we try to keep signs to a minimum. That way people have to ask questions and get into conversations. It's about getting people to talk to each other. Mind you, we've been beaten now with the toilets, I think we'll probably have to put up a sign."
Rhondda Pierre

Smoked haddock, cod & leek pie @ savoy
Pumpkin, mushroom & ricotta lasagna @ salad & ciabatta 8.50
Chargrilled organic burger @ pesto mayo, ciabatta Potato Wedges & Salad 7.50
Citrus marinated chicken breast @ basmati rice & creme fraiche 7.90
Pan fried halloumi @ mint dressing & chargrilled courgette salad 3.90/5.90
LEMON MARENGUE, MOCHA TORTE, PARSNIP CAKE, CARROT CAKE 2.90
a 12.5% service charge will be added to your bill for tables of 6 or more
drink
hubbub
4 IN A ROW
CHESS
SCRABBLE

269 Westferry Road
London E14 3RS

The Isle of Dogs is not a fertile ground for cafés with individual character. The architecture of Canary Wharf may be impressive, but the high rents ensure that only the usual chains are able to establish their facsimiles in the business district. However, a few stops further south on the Docklands Light Railway, Hubbub is the very antithesis of corporate, high-rise glamour. Housed upstairs in a former Presbyterian church on Westferry Road that is now The Space arts centre, it is a laid back, cosy café-bar, complete with sofas, a fish tank and an ever-changing menu of home-cooked food.

'I love the place, it is like my own front room. We've had my fish there for about seven months.'
Maura Ireland, Proprietor

"I can **walk** here in about twenty seconds, so if I get **peckish** you can always find me here. Occasionally, I **drive**. It takes longer but it is less effort."
James, Customer

"A lot of people don't know that this is here, but once they have **discovered** it they keep coming back. It's got the same sort of feel as a bar by the **beach** – it doesn't feel like London at all. It's a home away from home, everything about it is **chilled** out." Louise Roberts, Customer

'It is easy to forget that we're only 50 yards from the **river**. At high tide you can walk outside and see the **ships** going past.'
Gordon Silverman, Chef and Proprietor

'We made up our own **cocktails**. These ones were invented on a drunken evening. **Tinker** is our cat at home, **Misty** is Gordon's mum and dad's dog, and **Coco** is my mum's dog. We still think it is funny when people come up to the bar and say: 'Can I have two Tinkers please?' **Maura Ireland**

"We change our **breakfast** special every weekend: because we've got so many **regulars**, we don't want them getting bored. Maura came up with the idea of green eggs and ham, from **Dr Seuss**, so we put spinach and parsley in the scrambled egg. It is a bit of a **gimmick** really – but people are actually ordering it."
Gordon Silverman

St Paul's Presbyterian **church** was designed by T E Knightly and built in 1859. It catered to the Scottish **shipbuilders** working nearby at Burrells Wharf, the shipyard that built Brunel's Great Eastern. It ceased to be used as a church in 1972 and for a while was used by a neighbouring firm to test **crane** components. In 1989 it was taken over by the St Paul's Arts Trust and has been completely renovated. As **The Space**, it now hosts a wide range of performances, from **comedy** and cabaret to **classical** recitals, **jazz** and dance events.

Smoked Haddock, Cod and Leek Pie *serves 6*

Topping

1kg (2lb 4oz) potatoes, boiled and mashed
25g (1oz) butter
60ml (2 fl oz) cream
pinch of nutmeg
2 eggs, beaten

Filling

500g (1lb 2oz) cod fillet
500g (1lb 2oz) smoked haddock
900ml (1½ pints) milk
1 bay leaf
75g (2¾oz) butter
1 large leek, sliced
75g (2¾oz) flour
2 tablespoons chopped dill
2 tablespoons chopped parsley
juice of ½ lemon
salt and pepper

"The portions are always big – one of my pet hates is small portions – and we don't go in for big flowery descriptions." Gordon Silverman

+

savoy cabbage to serve
parsley to garnish

Preheat the oven to 200C (400F/gas mark 6). Mix the hot mashed potato with the butter, cream, nutmeg and beaten egg, reserving a little egg for glazing. Poach the fish for a few minutes in the milk with the bay leaf until almost cooked. Strain the milk and reserve. Pick through the fish for skin and bones and break into large chunks.

Melt the butter in a saucepan and sauté the leek until soft. Add the flour to make a paste then gradually add the milk to make a white sauce and cook for a few minutes to thicken. Add the fish, chopped herbs and lemon juice. Season to taste with salt and pepper.

Place the filling in a buttered baking dish and cover with potato topping. Brush with beaten egg. Bake in the preheated oven until the topping is golden brown. Serve with savoy cabbage and garnish with parsley.

"Sometimes we do **Irish** breakfast with soda bread and **black pudding**. And we do the hangover breakfast: that comes with a Bloody Mary or a **vodka** shot. At the weekend we do tend to get a few people coming in with **hangovers** – and sometimes people who haven't even been to bed." Maura Ireland

"We're doing **porridge** today. We put it on because of the miserable **weather**." Gordon Silverman

We had a **customer** come in and I asked him how he had found us. And he said he had heard the people in front of him on the **bus** whispering about Hubbub. So I think we're a really well kept secret on the **Isle of Dogs** – only people in the know know about us. Maura Ireland

"There isn't an **average** type of person round here. It is a **weird** area: it used to be **rough** but now you get quite a few business people, but when they come in here they're in **plain** clothes." Phin, Waiter

Parsnip and Fig Cake   serves 8

(recipe from Eamonn Sweeney, 4&twenty Bakery, Camberwell)

120ml (4 fl oz) vegetable oil	<u>Topping</u>
175ml (6 fl oz) milk	apricot jam
2 eggs	175g (6oz) icing sugar
1 tablespoon treacle	2 tablespoons water
115g (4oz) light soft brown sugar	2 tablespoons lemon juice
280g (10oz) wholemeal self-raising flour	
2 teaspoons mixed spice	+
175g (6oz) raisins	cream to serve
175g (6oz) dried figs	strawberries and kiwi to decorate
225g (8oz) parsnips, grated	cinnamon for dusting

Preheat the oven to 180C (350F/gas mark 4). Mix together the first five ingredients and set aside. Sift the flour and mixed spice into a mixing bowl and add any bran which may be left in the bottom of the sieve. Remove the hard stalks from the figs and chop them finely, then add to the mixing bowl with the raisins. Add the wet ingredients and mix thoroughly. Lastly mix in the grated parsnip, then transfer the mixture to a greased and lined 8-inch cake tin. Bake in the centre of the preheated oven for about 1 hour or until firm and golden brown. Turn out on to a wire rack to cool. To finish, brush the cooled cake with warm apricot jam, then mix the icing sugar, water and lemon juice together and pour over the cake. Serve the cake with fresh cream, decorated with strawberries and kiwi slices and dusted with cinnamon.

'Some people say to me: 'Don't you get horribly healthy working in a place like this?'
I say: 'No – we always have the weekend.' André Polo, Assistant Manager
JUS

Jus Cafe

30–32 Fouberts Place
London W1F 1HF

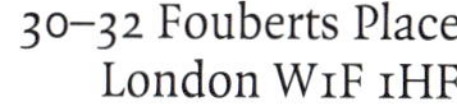

You can buy a coffee at the Jus Cafe, but coffee is not what the Jus Cafe is about. Here, just around the corner from Carnaby Street, the centre of attention is on juice drinks and smoothies. Browsing through the selection of fruit and vegetables on offer, even the most hardened caffeine addict is sure to find something that takes his or her fancy. But the Jus Cafe is no mere juice bar; it offers its customers a range of sandwiches, salads, snacks and desserts and invites them to take time out and linger upstairs in its bright and stylish seating area.

"It is not always that easy trying to start the juice bar concept in London. Not in a country with this particular climate and a population obsessed with drinking coffee."
Phil Howard, Director

96

'This guy magazine rang me up the other day and wanted to know which of our drinks were good aphrodisiacs. I said the main ones were carrot, apple, fennel and ginger: because the ginger increases your circulatory sector and it is meant to be able to produce endured muscle function. And the smoothie was the passion fruit, cherry and banana: the cherry is a real kind of mood enhancer, and so is banana, and passion fruit kind of speaks for itself. Alun Hund, Managing Director'

Phil Howard also owns The Square restaurant on Bruton Street in Mayfair and the Jus Cafe has two further branches on New Row in Covent Garden and on Kingsway in Holborn.

"We have **booster** shots that you can add to our standard menu. If you've got a **cold** or flu, **bee pollen** is brilliant. If you need an energy boost you can take **ginseng** or guarana. And ginger has got so many attributes it is **ridiculous**."
Alun Hund

"Ninety-nine per cent of us still **wake up** in the morning and our automatic **reaction** is to drink tea or **coffee** – but we're trying to **change** all that." Phil Howard

"The booster shots are **popular**. But some people just come in and take them once they've got a cold. That doesn't do you much **good**. But if you take them **regularly** they really do work." André Polo

Strawberry and Vanilla Smoothie

per serving

Strawberry syrup
500ml (18 fl oz) water
500g (1lb 2oz) sugar
100g (3½ oz) strawberries

Smoothie
vanilla yogurt
200g (7oz) strawberries
50ml (1¾ fl oz) cranberry juice
50ml (1¾ fl oz) strawberry purée

Make the strawberry syrup by heating the ingredients together in a large saucepan until the sugar has dissolved, then boiling rapidly for 5 minutes. When cool, liquidize the syrup. Make swirls of yogurt around the inside of a tall glass using a squeezy bottle, or by tipping the glass and spooning the yogurt around the inside. Place 3–4 ice cubes in an electric blender, add the strawberries, cranberry juice, strawberry purée and 50ml (1¾ fl oz) of the strawberry syrup and process until smooth. Pour the smoothie into the glass and serve.

"What makes a smoothie is the fact that all the ingredients are blended rather than juiced, everything is emptied into a container with a little bit of ice – it gives it a really smooth kind of consistency. And we don't use any milk in any of our smoothies – which a lot of places do to thicken them up. If it needs to be thickened up we just use banana with it, or coconut milk or maybe vanilla." Alun Hund

"The **customers** are a real **mixed bag**. My father comes in every day. He's a 60-year-old ex-**City** guy, and he loves it."
Phil Howard

'We wanted a **nature** aspect to run right through the café. The wooden **cutlery** is imported from Switzerland and it is made of **recycled** wood pulp. And the floor and table tops are washed **pebbles** covered with resin – and it is **safe** as well: it is non-slip.'
Alun Hund

"What we are trying to do is provide an **environment** in which you can get away from the **rat race** and sit down and enjoy something that is **healthy** and delicious – most importantly **delicious**. We're not trying to ram health down people's throats at the expense of enjoyment. We still do **chocolate mousse** and tiramisu. Anything in moderation is healthy – absolutely everything – and a little bit of chocolate mousse can go a long way: it certainly helps the **spirit**." Phil Howard

5-a-Day *per serving*

150g (5½oz) pineapple
150g (5½oz) cucumber
100g (3½oz) celery
1 apple
250g (9oz) carrot

Press all of the ingredients through a fruit and vegetable juicer to make a deliciously refreshing juice.

'I have a blender at home but I'm too lazy to use it – all that peeling and chopping.
André Polo'

Don't be
afraid: there may be
something a little medical about the
racks of vacuum-packed bags, but the innovative
system at the Jus Cafe is simplicity itself. Each bag contains
the perfect combination of ready chopped and peeled fruit and
vegetables to make your desired juice drink or smoothie.
Simply take it to the counter where the staff will
press or blend it for you.

Lounge

88 Atlantic Road
London SW9 8PX

The brainchild of actor Maynard Eziashi, Lounge is a welcome addition to the Brixton scene. Situated at the far end of Atlantic Road, it is a chilled-out and fashionable haven with laid back, modern design and friendly, easy going service. It is no surprise that it has become a second home to local artists and DJs who stop by regularly to sample the extensive range of juices and smoothies, the toasted sandwiches and the white hot chocolate.

> I used the **colours** to create the **atmosphere**. For me the **purple** is really key – it's a shame this book is in black and white. **Maynard Eziashi**

Maynard Eziashi originally conceived of the **idea** of a café back in 1991, but **film commitments** prevented him from starting Lounge until **early 1999**. He still manages to combine running **Lounge** with a successful film career.

"Lounge is really an **amalgamation** of all the cafés I have been to. I lived in **LA** for two years and I really liked the **café scene** over there – most **actors** hang out in cafés anyway most of the time – and I thought it would be good for **London**." Maynard Eziashi

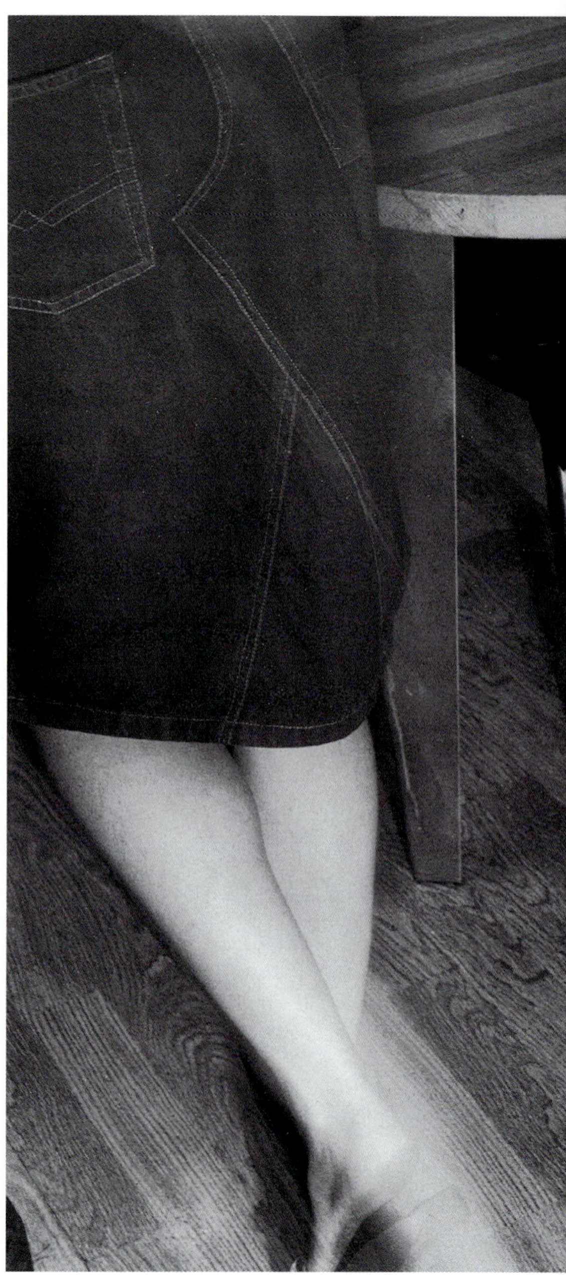

'I very rarely leave **Brixton**. I don't feel like I live in a city, I feel like I live in a **village**. We have everything we need here: a **cinema**, **shops**, **cafés** and **clubs**.'
Steven Preston, Manager

"This area used to be the front line. It was round here that the riots started. Over the road there used to be a community centre and all the shop fronts here were boarded up."

Maynard Eziashi

"The juices are really popular. We carry twelve different kinds of fruits, so the combinations are pretty much endless. It takes nearly a kilo of carrots to make one glass of juice, but it is worth it because the stuff is delicious."

Steven Preston

Customers at Lounge can also surf the net and check their e-mail at two computer terminals mounted on an ingenious, space-saving wall bracket made of scaffolding poles.

'It is really fun working here. And Stockwell Park is only down the road and they have a skate park over there. I go skating every day after work. It's wicked.

Kaori Sato, Waitress

Carrot and Coriander Soup

serves 2

4–6 carrots, chopped
1 onion, finely chopped
1 vegetable stock cube
1 tablespoon dried coriander
1 litre (1 3/4 pints) water
a splash of milk
25g (1oz) fresh coriander, chopped
nutmeg, salt and pepper
toasted ciabatta to serve

Place the carrots, onion, stock cube, dried coriander and water in a large saucepan and bring to the boil. Simmer gently until the carrots are soft. Add a splash of milk and half of the fresh coriander, then season with nutmeg, salt and pepper to taste. Pour the soup into a blender and blend until smooth. Pour into warmed soup bowls, garnish with the remaining coriander and serve with lightly toasted ciabatta.

"You don't have to have a **tattoo** to work here, but it does help. I think Ruth is pretty clear at the moment but everyone else has one in some shape or form. Perhaps I should make it part of my **selection criterion**. I could put it on the application form: 'Do you have a tattoo? And if not, why not?' "

Steven Preston

Crunchy Peanut Butter, Bramble Jelly and Banana Toasted Sandwich

per serving

1 large granary roll
butter
bramble jelly (or your favourite jam)
crunchy peanut butter
1 banana
strawberry and kiwi to decorate
½ teaspoon clear honey

Split the roll in half and lightly toast both sides. Butter the bottom half of the roll and spread generously with bramble jelly. Spread the top half of the roll with a generous helping of peanut butter.
Peel and thinly slice the banana; set aside a few slices for decoration. Arrange the remaining slices on top of the bramble jelly, then place the top of the roll back on top and cut in half. Place the sandwich on a plate and arrange the remaining banana slices, the strawberry and kiwi next to it. Drizzle the fruit with the honey and serve at once.

"The **peanut butter** sandwich is very **popular**. I wasn't sure that it would be because it is very **American**, but a lot of people seem to have taken to it."
Maynard Eziashi

lounge
COFFEE BAR

Quite who is responsible for building The Orangery is a matter of some debate. The design has been attributed variously to Sir Christopher Wren, Nicholas Hawksmoor and Sir John Vanbrugh. The initial estimate for the work was £2,599. Its final cost was £6,126.

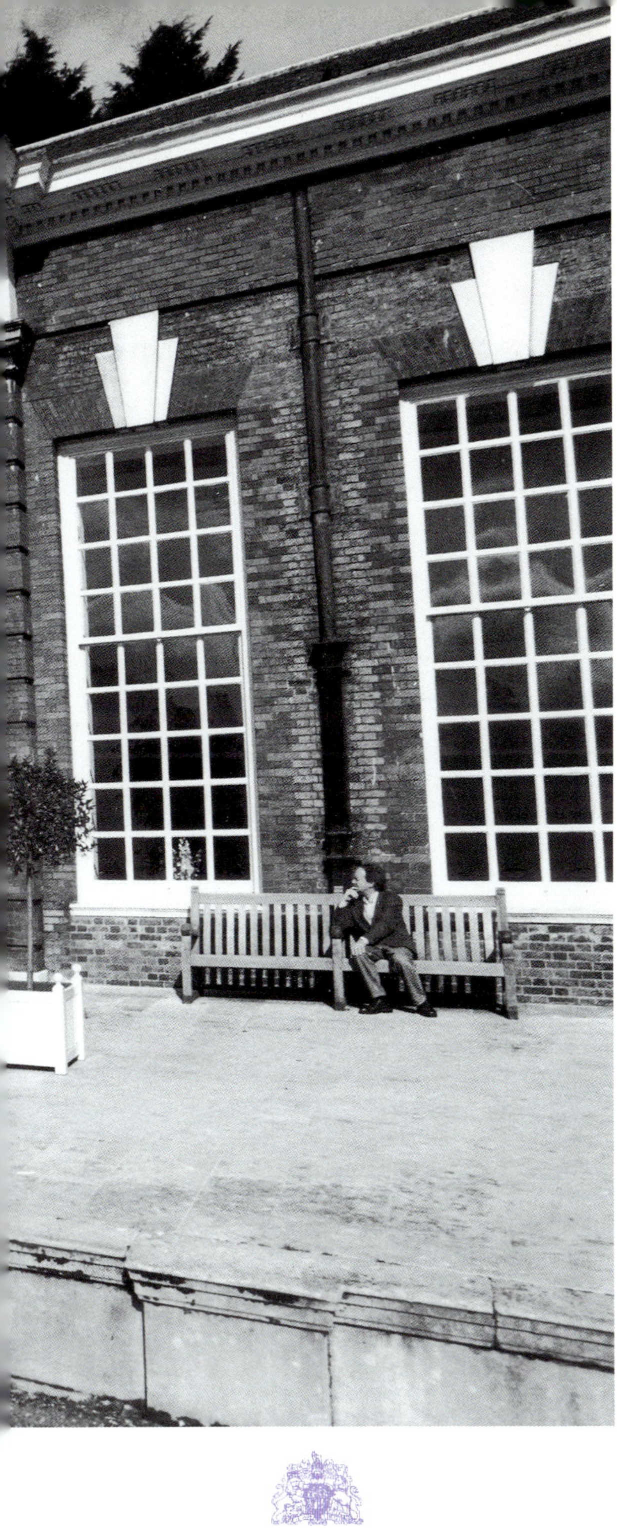

The Orangery

Kensington Palace
Kensington Gardens
London W8 4PX

There can be few more imposing spaces in London to enjoy lunch or afternoon tea than The Orangery at Kensington Palace. The vast, airy space – originally known as the greenhouse – was built for Queen Anne in 1704–5. During the winter months it was used for housing plants, and during the summer for court entertainments. Today The Orangery serves food all year round, though the orange trees from the terrace are still brought inside when the weather gets cold.

The chairs in The Orangery were designed by Historic Royal Palaces' curatorial department in period style but using modern materials.

"They weigh a ton, but they are absolutely gorgeous. They look like they come from Heal's and I want them in my house. I always say that if there are any missing they are in my dining room." Charlotte Baker, Historic Royal Palaces

As part of Kensington Palace, The Orangery is administrated by the charity Historic Royal Palaces. A memorandum of understanding with the Royal Household permits twenty corporate and charitable functions to take place in The Orangery every year.

'When you are a waitress here, the important thing is to have really good shoes – the floors are very hard and you have to walk such a long way.
Cecile Marchand, Chef

"Everything we do has to 'safeguard the status and dignity of Kensington Palace', and so we have to be very careful."
Charlotte Baker

"When I first walked in I thought it was far too posh for me. But once I began working here I started to love it."
Cecile Marchand

Orangery Cake serves 8–10

Cake

200g (7oz) butter
200g (7oz) caster sugar
grated zest of 2 oranges
pinch of salt
4 eggs, beaten
200g (7oz) self-raising flour, sifted

Orange Chiffon Icing

200g (7oz) full-fat soft cheese
juice and grated zest of 1 orange
400g (14oz) icing sugar
50g (1¾oz) unsalted butter,
    melted and cooled

Preheat the oven to 180C (350F/gas mark 4). To make the cake, cream the butter and sugar together until light and fluffy, using an electric blender if you like. Next add the grated orange zest and the salt. Add about a quarter of the beaten egg and mix well to incorporate, then add a little of the flour and mix again. Continue to add a little more beaten egg then a little more flour alternately until all the ingredients are incorporated and the mixture is smooth.

Grease and line a deep 8-inch cake tin and pour the mixture into it. Lightly smooth the surface, then place the tin in the preheated oven and bake for 40 minutes until the cake is well risen and lightly browned. Turn the cake out on to a wire rack to cool.

To make the icing, beat the cheese until smooth, then add the orange juice and zest and beat again to incorporate. Gradually fold in the icing sugar, then add the cooled butter and mix well to make a smooth icing.

Split the cooled cake across the middle into three pieces and use half of the Orange Chiffon Icing to sandwich the three pieces back together. Place the cake on a serving plate and cover the top and sides with the remaining icing.

Neither **dogs** nor **photography** are permitted in The Orangery.

" We did have these two **ladies** who brought in these tiny little **dogs** in their **handbags** – it was only when they were paying that we realized. That is really **illegal**. **Stuart Clark**, Manager **"**

Running a café in an **historic** building has its **disadvantages**: the kitchen is tiny, there is very limited storage space, deliveries are not permitted during the day, and in winter the **heating** is virtually **non-existent**.

"There are four ancient **radiators**, and they are useless. So in the winter you just have to **appreciate** the **building**."

Stuart Clark

Spiced Apple Cake   *serves 8*

Cake

450g (1 lb) apples
125g (4½oz) butter
300g (10½oz) caster sugar
a few drops of vanilla essence
1½ teaspoons cinnamon
¾ teaspoon nutmeg
¾ teaspoon mixed spice
½ teaspoon ground cloves

60g (2oz) raisins
3 eggs, beaten
350g (12oz) self-raising flour
1½ teaspoons baking power

Topping

60ml (2 fl oz) lemon juice
60g (2oz) caster sugar
cream or crème fraîche to serve

Cut one of the apples in half, set aside half of it for decoration and peel and chop the remaining apples. Place them in a saucepan with a little water and stew until they have softened. Remove from the heat. Preheat the oven to 180C (350F/gas mark 4). Cream the butter and sugar together until light and fluffy, then stir in the vanilla essence, the spices and the raisins. Add about a quarter of the beaten egg and mix well to incorporate, then add a little of the flour and the baking powder and mix again. Continue to add a little more beaten egg then a little more flour alternately until they are both incorporated and the mixture is smooth. Finally stir in the stewed apples and mix again. Pour the mixture into a greased and lined 8-inch cake tin. Peel and thinly slice the reserved half apple and arrange the slices on top of the cake. Sprinkle the apple slices with the lemon juice, then with the sugar. Bake the cake in the preheated oven for about 1 hour until well risen and lightly browned. A skewer inserted into the centre of the cake should come out clean. Remove the cake from the tin and place on a wire rack to cool. Serve the cake with whipped cream or crème fraîche.

The Orangery

"We set out to use everything we could that was **sustainable**, so the floor is from an old **gym**, the wood is storm oak from the trees that blew down in the great **storm**, the paint is natural **pigment** and we've got chicken-wire lights." **Carol Charlton**, Director

The Organic Café

25 Lonsdale Road
London NW6 6RA

London's first organic café started its life as a stall in the organic market at Camden. Since then – like the organic movement itself – it has considerably increased in size. In 1997 it moved to a large and unlikely site among light industrial units on a private road in Queens Park and has gone from strength to strength, receiving numerous accolades for its excellent food. But it is not just because of its organic status: in The Organic Café Carol Charlton has created a splendidly spacious and relaxed environment, whether you are dropping in for breakfast or a mid-morning coffee, or settling in for an evening meal.

> It started because I was working as an **environmental** consultant researching pesticides and health, advising supermarkets who said they were going to go **green** and never doing it. And I thought: I don't want to be sitting behind a computer – I want to be out there making it **happen**. Luckily, my family agreed to get involved too.
>
> Carol Charlton

"It can get a bit **crazy** in here at lunch. People always come in at the **same** time. It's always like that, it is as if they have been **awakened** or something." Gisele Torres, Waitress

"**Breakfast** on Sunday is a big thing. It is nice and **relaxed**. You can sit and read the papers and you don't feel rushed." Louise Purser, Customer

"We are registered and monitored by the Soil Association and they also monitor all our suppliers. You get accountability all the way through – and you don't get that in any other food chain. No way would you know where your food came from if it wasn't organic."
Carol Charlton

"I don't come in here because it is organic. I come in here because it is a nice place to sit. I think most people come in here because it is a nice atmosphere."
Louise Purser

The Organic Café has regular live music on Tuesday nights, jazz every Sunday and occasional opera evenings. Next door, the Organic Café Gallery is available to hire for exhibitions and private events.

'At night it is much more fancy. It is darker, and with all the fairy lights it looks like Christmas.'
Maggie Breheny, Waitress

Carol Charlton is the author of the **Organic Café Cookbook** and *Family Organic*. There are three Organic Café Cookshops and the latest project is the **Natural Homestore** in Notting Hill Gate.

'We are trying to extend the **organic** option, because you can actually live a sustainable **lifestyle**. People say you can't get the alternative mothball or the alternative paint, but you can if you look hard enough. People have begun to think about organic food, but they haven't thought about the chemicals we use in the house. They will **spray** anything round the room without reading the label, or wash their children's hair with toxic nit shampoo – and use other things that contain harmful **chemicals**.'

Carol Charlton

"I'm a **local** and I can remember when The Organic Café wasn't here. I must have been one of their **first** customers. I came in here a few days after it opened."

James Tyrrell, Customer

Feta Salad with Roasted Tomatoes and Parmesan Polenta   serves 4

Polenta

500g (1lb 2oz) polenta, cooked to packet
    instructions
100g (3½oz) butter
100g (3½oz) Parmesan cheese, grated
salt and white pepper
flour for dusting
olive oil for frying

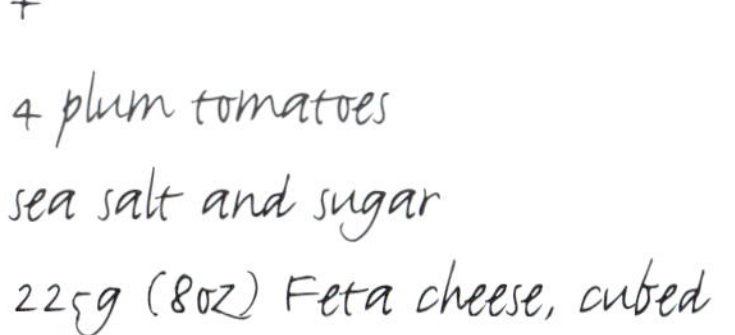

+

4 plum tomatoes
sea salt and sugar
225g (8oz) Feta cheese, cubed

rocket and basil leaf salad
vinaigrette dressing
1 teaspoon balsamic vinegar or
    1 teaspoon chopped capers

Preheat the oven to 120C (275F/gas mark 1). Cut the tomatoes in half and place in an ovenproof dish. Drizzle with a little olive oil and sprinkle with sea salt and sugar. Roast in the oven until half-dried and slightly blackened around the edges.

Mix the freshly cooked polenta with the butter, Parmesan and seasoning. Turn it out on to a greased surface and spread out to about 2.5cm (1in) thick. Leave to cool then use a sharp knife to cut it into 2.5cm (1in) squares. Heat a little olive oil in a frying pan, dust the polenta squares with a little flour then fry until crisp and brown on both sides. Drain on kitchen paper and season with pepper.

Mix the vinaigrette with the balsamic vinegar or capers, then use to dress the rocket and basil leaves. Divide the salad between the plates, then top with the polenta, Feta and roasted tomatoes. Serve immediately.

Thai Fishcakes and Chilli Noodles   serves 4–5

40g (1½oz) shallots, finely chopped
40g (1½oz) ginger, finely chopped
40g (1½oz) garlic, finely chopped
40g (1½oz) coriander leaves
15g (½oz) tarragon leaves
1 tablespoon sesame seeds, lightly toasted
1 tablespoon ground coriander
1 tablespoon turmeric
1 red chilli, deseeded and finely chopped
1 tablespoon peanuts or cashews
2 tablespoons sesame oil
shoyu or tamari sauce to taste
225g (8oz) organically farmed salmon
225g (8oz) cod, haddock or coley

Noodles

225g (8oz) dried noodles
chilli oil
sweet soy sauce
handful of coriander and basil leaves

Chilli Relish

225g (8oz) tomatoes, chopped
1 red chilli, deseeded and
   finely chopped
sweet vinaigrette dressing

+

vegetable oil for frying

Whizz all the ingredients for the fishcakes, except the fish, together in a blender until they form a slightly sticky paste, then stir-fry the paste in a wok for about 1 minute and tip into a mixing bowl. Debone and chop the fish finely with a large knife, then work it into the paste with your fingers.

Divide the mixture into small balls and pat flat. Pan fry in a little vegetable oil until browned and crisp on both sides. Take care not to burn them. Drain and keep warm. Soak the noodles according to packet instructions until soft. Mix with a little chilli oil, sweet soy and the herbs and toss in a hot pan with 2 tablespoons of water until well heated through. Mix all the ingredients for the Chilli Relish. Serve the fishcakes with the noodles and relish.

Use **organically** farmed salmon to make these fishcakes, as **wild** salmon is now an **endangered** species and ordinary **farmed** salmon is treated with **pesticides**.

'Cooking is really intimate. After sex it is the most intimate thing you do. You are putting things into your mouth for Christ's sake! It is incredibly intimate – and I feel a terrible responsibility.'

Alex Blee, Proprietor

The Quiet Revolution

49 Old Street
London EC1V 9HX

On the edge of the City in a former Post Office administrative building in between Shoreditch and Clerkenwell on the bleakest stretch of Old Street may not seem like the ideal location for an organic café – but then The Quiet Revolution is not really what you would expect an organic café to be. It is the simplest of spaces, and in its simplicity it succeeds in being both severe and accommodating. Its blank walls, clear lines and large low tables focus the attention precisely where it is supposed to be – on the food.

127

"There are **two ways** of doing anything. You can do exhaustive surveys and get '**professionals**' in to give you your concept and tell you where the next big **trend** is going to be. You can do that, and that is valid. Or – out of **conviction** in your own opinion – you can do what you believe in. That's what we do." Alex Blee

6 People automatically **assume** that we are 100 per cent vegetarian and that we are going to wear Jesus **sandals**, but we're not: we have really lovely ham and beef **stew**. And I think people are quite pleasantly **surprised** when they come in and realize that. Claire Plover, Manager **9**

"One customer said they wanted **air conditioning**. So I opened the doors for them. We aim to **please**." Helen Lowe, Waitress

"I **love** the kitchen. If I am **stressed** or anything, just get me peeling **spuds**. I am never unhappy when I am in the kitchen. Alex Blee**"**

The system of **service** at The Quiet Revolution is simplicity itself: the day's menu is displayed on removable **boards** hung behind the counter. You place your order at the **counter** and are given a number, and when your food is ready it will be delivered to your **table**.

All the **recipes** served at The Quiet Revolution are certified organic by the **Soil Association**.

"The **wheat grass** is very popular. It is a really amazing colour. It is bright **green** and when you first see it you think: 'Oh my God it looks like **bile**.' But it is actually quite **pleasant**. It is quite sweet and it tastes just how you imagine grass to taste." Claire Plover

What **impresses** me are the number of people who have been coming here from day one who didn't **realize** it was an organic café. And now they are actually seeking out **organic** food, so the **quiet revolution** – in its true meaning – is coming to fruition. Claire Plover

"It is not complicated, we just try to make a little more **effort** on every aspect, on every detail – that is what it is." Alex Blee

"We have the most amazing **salt**. It comes from the Ile de Re on the French coast near **Fort Boyard**. It is the finest salt in the world. It is great, it isn't bleached and it comes in great big **crystals**." Alex Blee

Ginger and Apple Chutney   makes 2kg (4½lb)

6 apples, peeled, cored and sliced

125g (4oz) onions, sliced

3 small dried chillies, chopped

2.5cm (1 inch) piece of fresh root ginger,
   peeled and sliced

2 tablespoons mustard seeds

1 garlic clove, sliced

2 teaspoons turmeric

90g (3oz) sultanas

200ml (7 fl oz) cider vinegar

150g (5½oz) sugar

Place all the ingredients in a stainless steel saucepan, bring to the boil, then turn down the heat and simmer gently for about 2 hours. Allow to stand overnight before serving. Store any leftover chutney in sterilized airtight jars.

At The Quiet Revolution organic **principles** extend well beyond the food: all the **water** is filtered and even the **electricity** comes from renewable resources.

"Do you like the **pinnies**? They are my homage to **David Beckham**." Alex Blee

Winter Onion Soup *serves 5*

1kg (2lb 4oz) organic white onions, sliced
100g (3½oz) organic butter
50g (1¾oz) organic rice miso
25g (1oz) organic tomato purée
½ teaspoon organic cayenne pepper
1½ litres (3½ pints) filtered water
1 tablespoon organic dry sherry
salt and pepper

Garnish
shavings of Penbryn cheese
garlic croûtons

Cook the onions gently in the butter for 45 minutes to 1 hour until they are soft and golden. Stir occasionally and do not allow the onions to burn. Add all the remaining ingredients and bring to the boil. Simmer for a few minutes, then serve hot garnished with cheese shavings and croûtons.

132

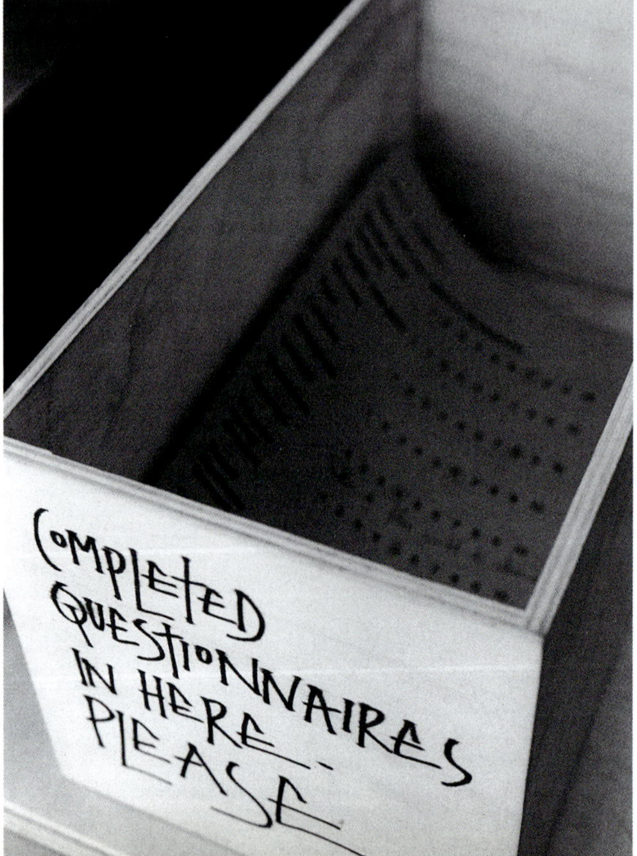

The Quiet Revolution
is always open to
suggestions
and invites
comments
from its customers.

> We take the **bad** ones out the back and **burn** them.
> Helen Lowe

We get everyone from Lordships to those who just want to celebrate something special.
Michael Kotb, Palm Court Manager

The Ritz

150 Piccadilly
London W1V 9DG

There is no more ravishing setting in London for afternoon tea than The Ritz. Here, in the lavish surroundings of the Palm Court, impeccably uniformed waiters deliver artfully arranged triple-decker racks of sandwiches, scones and cakes to elegantly decked tables. Surrounded by mirrors, marble columns, chandeliers and gilded trellises it is easy to imagine yourself back in the 1920s. But remember to be correctly attired as The Ritz has a dress code – men must wear a jacket and tie, and no jeans or trainers are allowed.

The Ritz London – the brainchild of the famous hotelier César Ritz – first opened in 1906. It was designed by Mewes and Davis in the style of a French château and was the first steel-framed building of any significance in London. It was meticulously restored in 1995 following a change of ownership.

There are three sittings for tea at The Ritz: at two o'clock, three-thirty and five o'clock. For the three-thirty and five o'clock sittings it is essential to book in advance but the two o'clock sitting is unreserved and during the week it is nearly always possible to find a table.

> People tend to regard the two o'clock sitting as a late lunch, and the five o'clock sitting is very popular as a filling pre-theatre meal.
>
> Andrew Jarman, Food and Beverage Manager

Keeping the **glittering** surroundings of the **Palm Court** up to scratch is an unrelenting task. Early in the morning the **flower** arrangements are rejuvenated and twice a day a member of The Ritz staff does the rounds replacing defective **bulbs**. He usually replaces between 70 and 80 bulbs a **day** and, in winter, due to the changing temperatures, as many as 150.

137

Mixed Fruit Tartelettes

makes 100

Sweet Paste

900g (2lb) butter
600g (1lb 5½oz) icing sugar
150g (5½oz) ground almonds
375g (13oz) eggs
1.5kg (3lb 6oz) plain flour
70g (2½oz) salt

Pastry Custard

1 litre (1¾ pints) milk
250g (9oz) caster sugar
200g (7oz) egg yolks
90g (3oz) powdered cream
100g (3½oz) whipped cream
90g (3oz) dohler fond

200 strawberries, halved
17 kiwis, sliced
300 blueberries
20 peaches, sliced
9 starfruits, sliced

Preheat the oven to 180C (350F/gas mark 4). To make the pastry, cream together the butter and the sugar until smooth then add the almonds and eggs and mix again. Sift the flour and the salt into the mixing bowl and combine with the other ingredients to form a soft paste. Form into a ball and allow to rest in the refrigerator for at least an hour. To make the pastry cream, heat the milk and half the sugar gently until they reach boiling point. Whisk the egg yolks with the remaining sugar until light and fluffy, add the cream powder, then pour in the boiling milk. Whisk well, then return to the pan and simmer gently for four minutes. Allow to cool. Mix in the whipped cream and dohler fond. Roll out the pastry to about 5mm (¼in) thick and use to line 100 greased tartelette tins. Prick with a fork and bake for 15–20 minutes. Allow to cool, then pipe the pastry custard into the pastry cases. Top with a selection of fresh fruits, arranged artfully on the custard.

"We are always busy here. Last year I broke the record for all time: I did 264 teas in one afternoon."
Michael Kotb

"We get a lot of ladies who were brought here as children by their godmothers, and now they are bringing their own god children here." Andrew Jarman

"Our pianist used to play for Frank Sinatra. Every time Sinatra came to London he was hired to play with him, so he knows all his songs. In fact, he knows everything. People ask him for requests and he can always play them. At the weekends we have a harpist." Michael Kotb

"The sandwiches come on a variety of breads: sundried tomato bread, spinach bread, caraway bread and white bread. Some people say, 'What's this green sandwich?' And you have to explain to them that that is the spinach bread."
Alfie Perez, Head Waiter

Ritz Sandwiches

<u>Smoked Salmon Sandwiches</u>
brown bread
lemon butter
smoked salmon

<u>Cucumber Sandwiches</u>
spinach bread
dill butter
thinly sliced cucumber

<u>Ham Sandwiches</u>
tomato bread
sundried tomato butter
thinly sliced ham

<u>Cream Cheese Sandwiches</u>
caraway bread
cream cheese
finely snipped chives

<u>Egg Sandwiches</u>
white bread
mayonnaise
hard-boiled eggs, mashed

> **6** We
> have a lot of good
> **sandwiches**,
> and really good **cakes**.
> And it is **unlimited** as
> well. Guests often ask if they can
> take the cakes away with them,
> but we don't like to do that
> any more because they are
> **fresh cream**.
> Michael Kotb **9**

To make perfect finger sandwiches, slice the bread lengthways, remove the crusts and straighten the edges. Make up the large rectangular sandwiches with the ingredients above, then cut them into eight equal fingers.
Arrange one of each type of the five different sandwiches in a 'raft', to be served to each person. Continue to serve rafts of sandwiches until everyone is full.

S&M Café

268 Portobello Road
London W10 5TY

Tucked under the Westway on Portobello Road, S&M, the Sausage & Mash Café, is exactly what it says it is. With large tables and functional modern decor it serves up generous portions of wholesome, comfort food to the denizens of Notting Hill from eleven in the morning to ten o'clock at night. But S&M is no greasy spoon: the idea might be simple but the execution is friendly and accommodating, and with a regularly changing range of sausages, mashes and gravies it succeeds in adding an edge of sophistication to the most traditional of British dishes.

Choice is of the essence at S&M – as long as it is sausages. You choose your own combination from the daily range on offer, and add to that your selection of mash and gravy.

"The idea started when I was in New York for a weekend. I was Christmas shopping and it was one of those really cold days. And I thought: sod all these New York delis, what I want now is a plate of sausage and mash. But there wasn't anywhere to go. And then I thought: hang on, there is nowhere in England either. It is one of the most British meals you can get but there is nowhere that specializes specifically in sausage and mash."

Sarah Barton-Smith, Proprietor

' If you came here on 14 February you would be amazed. I tell you, if any boyfriend of mine brought me here for Valentines night, I would dump him. Sarah Barton-Smith '

"The first time I saw it I thought 'Ugh, sausage and mash and gravy.' But then I tried it and it was great. It is a great concept." Andy Clarke, Customer

"Some weeks we do more vegetarian sausages than we do meat. But then I guess vegetarians need to get their comfort food too." Dean Lister, Manager

"We get a lot of celebrities in here, and most of the time they are nicer than the general public." Renée Kere-Kere, Waitress

"Lots of people ask me who the **designer** was. The designer was me. I made it up as I went along. See that line on the pillar. It is a bit **wobbly** – that is where the masking tape didn't stick." Sarah Barton-Smith

"The first thing I did was buy the **chairs**. The whole thing came from the chairs. That is why the walls have green **stripes**. They are original **1930s** working men's club chairs and I found them in Leyton Buzzard in **Loot** for a tenner each." **Sarah Barton-Smith**

‘I **loved** this café so much that I came here all the time – and then they asked me if I wanted to **work** here.’
Renée Kere-Kere

Bruschetta of Wild Mushrooms with Grilled Halloumi *per serving*

25g (1oz) shallots, chopped
a little butter
50g (1¾oz) wild mushrooms
20g (¾oz) chopped chives
1 diagonal slice of French bread, toasted
2 slices of Halloumi cheese
salt and pepper
salad leaves to garnish

Sweat the shallots in the butter until soft. Add the mushrooms and cook gently for about 5 minutes or until done. Add the chives and season with salt and pepper. Arrange the freshly toasted bread on a large white plate and spoon the mushrooms on top. Grill the Halloumi until golden on both sides and lay on top of the bruschetta. Garnish with a few mixed salad leaves and sprinkle with chives. Serve hot.

All the sausages at S&M are made by Simply Sausages. All the meat contained in the sausages is produced under the RSPCA's Freedom Food programme which upholds farm animal welfare standards including farmer, haulier and processor.

"The tables had to be rebuilt after the carnival last year, because there were so many people dancing on them."
Sarah Barton-Smith

Sausages with Fennel and Dill Mash and Mushroom Gravy   *serves 4*

8 good quality sausages

Fennel and Dill Mash
1kg (2lb 4oz) potatoes
200g (7oz) melted butter
2 dessertspoons double cream
200g (7oz) bulb fennel, chopped
100g (3½oz) dill, chopped
salt and pepper

Mushroom Gravy
150g (5½oz) mixed leeks,
   onions, carrots and celery,
   finely chopped

1 sprig of thyme
1 sprig of rosemary
2 bay leaves
6 peppercorns
1 tablespoon vegetable oil
250ml (9 fl oz) white wine
450ml (¾ pint) red wine,
   reduced by half
50g (1¾oz) shallots, chopped
15g (½oz) butter
150g (5½oz) mushrooms, sliced
50g (1¾oz) tarragon, chopped
50g (1¾oz) tomatoes, peeled,
   deseeded and diced

To make the gravy, fry the mixed vegetables, thyme, rosemary, bay leaves and peppercorns in the oil until golden brown. Add the white wine and reduce by half over a high heat. Add the red wine and simmer for 30 minutes. Pass the gravy through a sieve and return to the pan. In a separate pan, sweat the shallots in the butter until soft, then add the mushrooms and cook for 5 minutes on a low heat. Drain and add to the gravy with the tarragon and tomatoes. Season well.

To make the mash, boil the potatoes and mash until totally smooth. Add the butter and cream and season well. Fry the fennel gently in a little butter until soft, then add to the mash with the dill.

Grill or fry the sausages, then serve with the mash and gravy.

> **I could talk about sausage and mash for England.**
> Sarah Barton-Smith

I was cleaning the fire-damaged altar *and I was inspired – it is a good place to get* inspiration: *cleaning an altar. Heidi Ektvedt, St Paul's* Volunteer

St Paul's Café

1 St Paul's Road
London N1 2QH

The nave of a nineteenth century church is certainly an unusual place to find a vegetarian café. But St Paul's Church, on the borders of Islington and Dalston, is no longer a conventional place of worship. For eight years it has been the home of the St Paul's Steiner Project and the café itself is part of an ambitious, on-going development to restore the building and convert it into an educational centre and theatre for the local community.

That the café should be **organic** should come as no surprise: Rudolph **Steiner** was one of the founding fathers of the modern organic movement.

St Paul's Church was built in 1826–8 by Sir Charles Barry who later went on to design the Houses of Parliament together with Augustus Pugin. Due to a declining congregation it was de-consecrated in 1982.

"This café represents a lot more than just a café trying to make money. As long as we break even it is fine. I could open at night, cut my portions, quadruple my prices, put candles on the tables and have mint leaves with everything; but I don't want to end up with a string of Range Rovers parked outside, that is not what this place is about."
David Sheffield, Chef

Apart form David Sheffield and his assistant all the **staff** at the St Paul's Café are **volunteers**; and in keeping with the educational purpose of the project both the café and the kitchen are used to provide work **experience** and culinary training.

Heidi Ektvedt, one of the **volunteers**, recently cycled from San Francisco to Mexico to raise money for the urgent **repairs** that are required to the roof of St Paul's Church. Her **website** can be visited at **www.rideforcover.org**.

'We all believe in **energy**. Don't be taken in by the short orange hair. Inside I've got **dreadlocks** down to my knees – and lots of **piercings** probably. Heidi Ektvedt

"I try to get out and see the **customers**. It is nice for me, and it is good for them to see the person who is **cooking**. We had this old guy who said: 'I'm 87 and I've been a vegetarian for 62 **years** and 6 months – and they said I'd be **dead** in 6 months when I started.' " David Sheffield

The St Paul's **Steiner** Project is an educational facility for all ages: it contains a kindergarten and a **school** as well as workshops for stonecarving, leaded window making and **welding**

I came here last year answering an **ad** *for a café manager. I looked at this place and thought: 'Sure, this could be a happening spot, what is the* **catch**? ' And they said: 'The catch is that you have got to* **build** *it first." So I did a lot of the building work here. I made the whole front garden, the front* **entrance** *and the floor and all the* **finishing**. David Sheffield

"I used to **live** here. I had to wear a **hard-hat** to bed and climb in through a hole in the wall. It was **fabulous**." Heidi Ektvedt

St Paul's must be one of the few cafés that has its own **compost heap**. "I like the connection with the **earth**. We put all our **raw** vegetable waste out here, but no cooked food – that attracts **rodents**."
Norah Meany, Assistant Manager

Thai-style Vegetable Flan   *serves 6–8*

<u>Vegetable Topping</u>
1 small red pepper, finely diced
2 spring onions, diagonally sliced
½ bunch fresh coriander
1 onion, diced
2 carrots, diced
1 broccoli floret, diced
4 large mushrooms, diced
1 lemon grass stalk, very finely chopped
1 tablespoon grated ginger
1 tablespoon grated garlic
1 tablespoon sesame oil
1 tablespoon white pepper and salt

<u>Crust</u>
225g (8oz) butter
450g (1lb) plain flour

<u>Filling</u>
175ml (6 fl oz) vegetable oil
175g (6oz) gram flour
950ml (1 pint 12 fl oz) vegetable stock
1 kaffir lime leaf, shredded

Preheat the oven to 200C (400F/gas mark 6). To make the crust, knead together the butter and flour until it forms a firm dough, then roll out on a floured surface and use to line a 10-inch nonstick flan tin. Trim the edges and set aside.

To make the filling, heat the oil in a saucepan, add the gram flour and stir to form a ball. Add a little of the stock and stir constantly, keeping the mixture just at boiling point. Continue to add the stock, a little at a time, until it has all been incorporated and the mixture is smooth. Add the lime leaf, season well and simmer for 5 minutes. Set aside. For the vegetable topping, set the spring onion, coriander and half the red pepper aside, then sauté all the other ingredients for about 5 minutes. The vegetables should stay crisp. To assemble the flan, pour the filling into the pasty case and spread it out. Sprinkle the vegetables on top, then garnish with the red pepper, spring onion and remaining coriander. Place in the preheated oven and bake for 45 minutes or until the pastry is cooked through.

St Paul's Nut Burgers *serves 6*

2 tablespoons vegetable oil

2 teaspoons sesame oil

2 small onions, finely diced

2 carrots, finely diced

1 green pepper, finely diced

1 red pepper, finely diced

3 garlic cloves, crushed

1 tablespoon grated fresh root ginger

900g (2lb) cooked aduki beans

120ml (4 fl oz) water

60ml (2 fl oz) tamari or soy sauce

handful of fresh coriander, chopped

115g (4oz) walnut halves

115g (4oz) pumpkin seeds

115g (4oz) sunflower seeds

225g (8oz) gram flour

salt and pepper

+

oil for frying

garlic toast

alfalfa sprouts

tomato slices

chutney

Heat the vegetable oil and sesame oil in a large pan and sauté all the diced vegetables, the garlic and the ginger, for about 5 minutes. They should remain crunchy.

Transfer them to a large bowl and add the beans, water, tamari, coriander, nuts and seeds. Mash the mixture together, season with salt and pepper, then add the gram flour to bind it and mix well. The mixture should be wet and sticky.

Form the mixture into burgers and fry in a little oil to brown on both sides. Once the burgers have been formed, they can be finished off in the oven, on a barbecue or under a grill. Cook until firm right through.

Serve the burgers on garlic toast, topped with alfalfa sprouts, sliced tomato and chutney.

The St Paul's Steiner Project website can be visited at **www.btinternet.com/~stpauls.**

'The Star is different. You are not going to get ripped off, the food is of exceptional quality, the portions are more than adequate, and it is fun. You can make millions selling burgers and pizzas and things like that, but you can only paint one Mona Lisa. And I'm not saying that we are a Mona Lisa – but then on the other hand, the value of the Mona Lisa is nothing compared to the fortunes of people who sell hamburgers. Mario Forte, Proprietor

The Star Café

22 Great Chapel Street
London W1V 3AQ

Possibly one of the best kept secrets in Soho — but no secret to anyone who works in the area – The Star Café has been packing in customers since 1933 with a reliable combination of good honest food, excellent coffee and a changing daily menu. Its extraordinary interior is a treasure in itself, with checked table cloths and every available inch of wall space covered with posters, old enamel signs and antique vending machines – even the ashtrays are collectors' items.

160

"There is nothing **false** about this place. Its **character** has developed since 1936. You can't impose character on a place if that character doesn't exist." **Jonathan Ransford**, Manager

"You meet a lot of people in here, **media** people and all sorts. They're a fun bunch. I'd be **bored** if I worked in an office." Alexandra, Waitress

"We get them all in here: film stars, **celebrities**, actors, directors. I've been here 29 years. I started in 1971, and I'm **60** this year so I'm **retiring** – I've had enough of it now." Rena Daly, Waitress

I specialize in **hangover** cures. Trust me – no matter how you feel, I can sort you out. I can tell what you need. Jonathan Ransford

Formerly a **pub**, a hairdressers and (allegedly) even a house of **ill repute**, the corner premises of The Star Café have been put to various **uses** over the years.

'When my **father** started here it was much smaller. It had four marble-top tables, **sawdust** on the floor, and one **pin-ball** machine in the corner. And it was very much egg and chips; sausage, egg and chips; and bacon, egg and chips. Mario Forte'

Because of its location in the heart of **Soho**, the vast majority of The Star's customers are involved in the **film** business in one capacity or another. Mario himself is also a co-owner of **Joe's Basement**, the professional film processing laboratory.

"Downstairs is the **non-smokers'** cave. We lock them in there, where they can breath fresh air in the dark." Alexandra

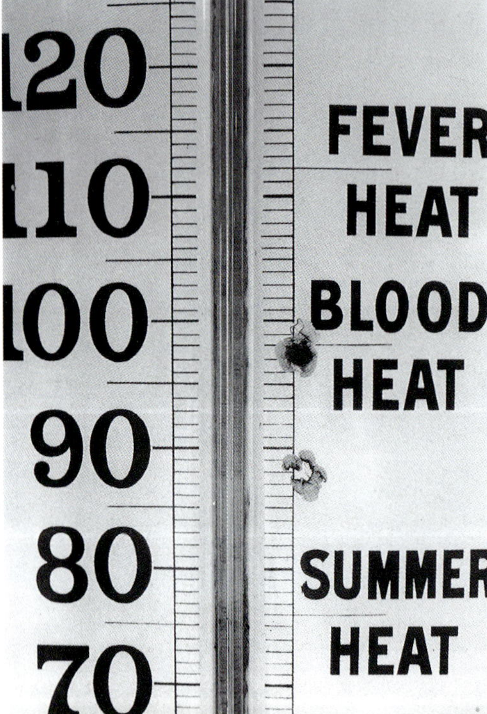

"It is honest caff food – when your food arrives you expect not to be able to see the plate. And you know you are going to leave here full. Unlike some restaurants where you pay double the price and as soon as you leave you have to go to McDonald's." Jonathan Ransford

Star Veggie Special *per serving*

½ red pepper, sliced

½ small onion, sliced

1 large tomato, sliced

1 portion ciabatta

1 tablespoon Neapolitan pasta sauce or

  1 teaspoon tomato purée

sliced Mozzarella

grated Cheddar cheese

4–6 basil leaves

Roast the peppers, onions and tomatoes on a baking tray in a hot oven or under a hot grill, until tender. Cut the ciabatta horizontally and toast the two halves. Spread the toasted ciabatta thinly with Neapolitan sauce or tomato purée. Cover the bottom slice with the roasted vegetables and Mozzarella, sprinkle with Cheddar cheese and grill until the cheese has melted. Sprinkle with fresh basil, replace the top and serve.

163

"We still do some of the **traditional puddings** like bread and butter **pudding** and apple tart, but we used to do some obscure ones, like **Cabinet** Pudding. No one else has ever heard of it, but I **grew up** with it – it was like a bread and butter pudding with the **custard** cooked into it."
Mario Forte

star Club sandwich *per serving*

3 slices of white bread, toasted
mayonnaise
Tabasco sauce
shredded lettuce
2 rashers of smoked bacon, grilled
4 slices of cooked chicken breast
sliced tomato
grated Cheddar cheese

Spread two slices of the toast with mayonnaise and Tabasco and cover with shredded lettuce. Top both of them with bacon, chicken, tomato and grated cheese and then microwave until the cheese has melted. Stack the two slices of toast on top of each other and finish off with the third slice to make a triple-decker sandwich. Cut in half and serve on a bed of lettuce.

The Star Café also does a *thriving* trade in take-away sandwiches

'When people come in here they get the sandwich they *want*. If they don't want butter, they don't get butter You can't do that in Prêt A Manger or Benjy's because they make them all up in advance. You can't say I don't like cucumber and I'm allergic to tomato. But here we make sandwiches by design. You design them and we make them. Jonathan Ransford'

Tate Modern Café

Sumner Street
London SE1 9TG

Tate Modern is nothing if not monumental and if it has one drawback, it is that it is too big. Whether you are here for the architecture or the art, or simply to enjoy the new vistas of London that the development of Bankside has thrown up, at some point your feet are going to tell you that you need a break. The architects, however, have been mindful of their visitors' plight. The café on the ground floor of Tate Modern is an integral part of the building; it is a bustling, busy, high-ceilinged space, full of straight lines and reflective surfaces and boasting magnificent views across the river.

"I think some of the customers get scared off when they look in and can't find a tray to run along those little rails." Andy Gordon, Assistant Manager

"When we **opened** at ten o'clock on 12 May we were full immediately and we had a **queue** of two hundred people outside. It was more **popular** than we expected it to be. In the end we had to control the **numbers** coming into the building." Duncan Ackery, Managing Director

168

I like it when it is **busy**. I used to work in a Spanish restaurant in the City; there was just two of us and we did **120** people for lunch. Now that was busy. You get a bit **addicted** to it. I couldn't work in a West End restaurant, it would be too slow. **Pedro Romero-Perez**, Waiter

"There's never a table **free** for more than half a minute at **lunchtime**. And some days we get all the **tour buses** in London – they dump everyone off here and it is **crazy**."
Willhelm Louw, Waiter

169

"The **philosophy** behind the **food** is that everything is made in house and we use the best quality ingredients. We don't want it to be **elitist** We want to have business people sitting next to families. We aim to please everyone."
Sean Davies, Executive Chef

' I bring my three-year-old in on **Sunday** mornings just to come and **annoy** them. She loves it. Her favourite work in the gallery is Cornelia Parker's **Cold Dark Matter**, the exploding shed. She's just mad about it. Mind you, I have had to stop her running at the **Mark Rothkos** with sticky hands. **'**
Duncan Ackery

"You can see from the positioning of this café, and of the café upstairs, that they gave us a great spot within the gallery. It is not like one of the Victorian buildings where you end up in the basement dodging pillars." Duncan Ackery

"Some people think that because we are in an art gallery we're going to be very posh, and then they come in here and think we're a bit of a caff. And other people expect a sandwich wrapped in cellophane and they are very impressed. But the idea is that whether you come in for a cappuccino or a bottle of champagne and a three course meal, you still get the same service."
Andy Gordon

In the beginning no one wanted to sit in this corner so we made it into the smoking section and now it is always full.
Arantxa Martinez, Waitress

"On the application form, when we as why people want work at Tate Modern, a lot of people put 'Because I want t be surrounded b art.' But I thin that wears off afte week or two beca you are surround by plates ar cutlery." Andy Gordon

Griddled Chicken with Spiced Lentil Salsa *serves 6*

6 chicken breasts
60ml (2 fl oz) olive oil
1 large garlic clove, crushed
a handful of coriander leaves

Spiced Lentil Salsa
1 red onion, finely chopped
40g (1½oz) fresh root ginger, finely chopped
2 garlic cloves, crushed
2 chillies, deseeded and finely chopped
1 tablespoon ground cumin
1 teaspoon cumin seeds
50ml (1¾ fl oz) water
75ml (3 fl oz) balsamic vinegar
250g (9oz) puy lentils, cooked

½ bunch of coriander, chopped
60ml (2 fl oz) chilli sauce
60g (2oz) sundried tomatoes, chopped
60g (2oz) tomato ketchup
3 tablespoons sweet soy sauce
50ml (1¾ fl oz) olive oil
salt and pepper

Marinate the chicken breasts in the olive oil, garlic and coriander overnight. To make the salsa, put the onions, ginger, garlic, chillies, ground cumin and seeds into a pan with the water and balsamic vinegar and simmer, covered, for 2 minutes. Remove from the heat and add all the remaining ingredients, mix well and refrigerate overnight. Place the chicken in a preheated hot griddle pan until cooked through, then serve with the salsa.

In keeping with its location, Tate Modern Café is also a showcase for modern **design**: the furniture is by **Jasper Morrison**, the crockery is a **Kaj Franck** design, and the waiters' and waitresses' uniforms are by **Sir Paul Smith**.

Apple and Blackberry Crumble   serves 4–5

50g (1³/₄oz) butter
600g (1lb 5¹/₂oz) apples, peeled
    and diced
125g (4¹/₂oz) sugar
40g (1¹/₂oz) ground cinnamon
175g (6oz) blackberries

+

icing sugar for dusting
thick cream or ice cream to serve

Custard Cream

3 egg yolks
60g (2oz) sugar
250ml (9 fl oz) double cream
¹/₄ vanilla pod

Topping

50g (1³/₄oz) butter
50g (1³/₄oz) sugar
100g (3¹/₂oz) flour

Preheat the oven to 200C (400F/gas mark 6). To make the apple mixture, melt the butter in a saucepan, add the apples, sugar and ground cinnamon and cook until soft; then add the blackberries. Place the mixture in an ovenproof dish and set aside. To make the topping, beat the butter and sugar together until well combined, then add the flour and continue to beat until the crumble starts to form. Arrange on top of the apple and bake in the oven until the crumble topping is golden.

To make the custard, whisk the egg yolks and sugar in a bowl until light and fluffy. Slowly bring the cream and vanilla pod to the boil, then pour on to the egg and sugar mixture and stir well. Return to the saucepan and cook gently until the custard coats the back of the spoon. Do not allow it to boil. Dust the crumble with icing sugar and serve with the custard cream, plus thick cream or ice cream.

'What is he **doing**? Waiting for the apple crumble to **smile**?'

Pedro Romero-Perez

VICTORY
CAFE
&
Milk
bar

Victory Café

26 South Molton Lane
London W1Y 2LP

Tucked away in the basement of Gray's Antique Market at the side of South Molton Street, the Victory Café is an oasis of quirky 1940s charm just a stone's throw from the bustle of Oxford Street. Multicoloured furniture clashes gorgeously with the vibrant carpet while the murals celebrate the end of austerity. And on the menu, traditional British breakfasts, and sausage and mash sit side by side with classic French salads and traditional Basque soup.

> Every day we get **new** customers; people come up from Mayfair, and we even get some **customers** because of the extractor fan: they smell the food from the nearby offices and just follow their noses.
>
> ## Steve Bungaroo
> Manager

175

The Victory Café and its nostalgic theme was the brainchild of Benny Gray, the owner of Gray's Antique Market. Before he renovated in 1998 it used to be a little old caff with bench seating.

The customers at the Victory Café range from antiques dealers from the market to office workers and students from Vidal Sassoon and the London College of Fashion.

"Lots of dealers come in here and have a cup of tea and deal. They make thousands of pounds, and we make one pound twenty." Monica Tinelli, Waitress

"There's nothing **1940s** about the food. No one has ever come in and asked for **Spam** or powdered eggs. But we don't only do things that are on the **menu**, so if someone did ask – and Andy could do it – he would do it."
Steve Bungaroo

"I'm a **regular**. They are really good and Andy will make whatever you like. They are **custom built** meals. If I ask for a little bit of cucumber on the side, he does it, when most people would think you are **raving mad**." Kirsty, Assistant Manager
Gray's Antique Market

177

'I try not to drink **coffee** during the day because I am **hyperactive** enough already.
Monica Tinelli'

"We don't want people to come here just to have a coffee. They can come here and sit down and have nothing, so long as they are happy. We want everybody to keep a smile as long as possible."
Steve Bungaroo

"A lot of older people come here and love the atmosphere. Not only that, they love the music as well and they make requests from the jukebox. It reminds them of the old times and they love it – but none of them has ever asked us for Spam." Steve Bungaroo

'You get used to working down here. It is a surprise at the end of the day when you go out and see what the weather is like. And in the morning I always walk from Oxford Circus just so I can see some daylight.'
Monica Tinelli

"We've only got one ashtray left, the rest of them had wings. I'll have to order some more." Steve Bungaroo

Basque Vegetable Soup *serves 6*

4 tablespoons olive oil

2 onions, roughly chopped

2 leeks, sliced

4 carrots, sliced

2 garlic cloves, chopped

1 large potato, cubed

400g (14oz) can chopped tomatoes

1 teaspoon sugar

1 litre (1³/₄ pints) water

½ head of endive, roughly torn

salt and pepper

Heat the oil in a large saucepan and fry the onions, leeks, carrots and garlic, without browning, until slightly softened. Add the remaining ingredients, cover the pan and bring to the boil. Reduce the heat and cook at a gentle simmer for 2–3 hours until the soup is rich and thick. This can be done on top of the stove or in the oven.

Chef Andrew Slaine is originally from Bedford but he spent **ten years** working in the **Pays Basque** and the French Alps.

"I went down there **backpacking** and just travelling around. I ended up in the Pays Basque and decided to **stay** for a few years." **Andrew Slaine**, Chef

' I do the same **soup** every day. In the Pays Basque we used to eat the same soup every day all year round. It is what you call a **soupe du soir**. The evening meal would be a bowl of soup with a bit of cheese and a yogurt. '

Andrew Slaine

Goats' Cheese Salad *per serving*

60g (2oz) goats' cheese
1 large slice country bread
2 large handfuls mixed salad leaves
2 tomatoes, cut into wedges
cucumber slices
vinaigrette dressing

Toast the country bread until crisp. Spread the goats' cheese thickly on the bread, then place under a preheated hot grill and toast until the cheese has melted. Meanwhile, arrange the salad leaves on a serving plate and arrange the tomato wedges and cucumber slices around the edges. Dress the salad with the vinaigrette. When the cheese has melted, cut the bread into small pieces and distribute evenly over the salad. Serve warm.

> They are really **accommodating**. I had been through everything on the menu and I wanted something **different**. So instead of having sausage, mushrooms and whatever, I just asked for egg, bacon and toast. And being a creature of **habit** I had that for about two weeks and everyone started calling it the **Hilary Special**. And then I changed to a sandwich with **chicken** and **cranberry sauce**, and now they call that the Hilary Special Two.
>
> Hilary, Customer

Babycha
VICTORY

I don't know what it is. Sometimes it is too noisy,
sometimes there are too many kids,
but there is something about it.
And they do the best coffee without a doubt. Kath Bilgora, Customer

The World Café

Nestling in between Muswell Hill and Finsbury Park, Crouch End is one of the most endearing areas of north London. Thanks to having no tube station of its own, it has retained a charming small-town feel, with a proper little high street and numerous independent shops. But even if you are not a local resident, The World Café makes the bus trip from Finsbury Park worthwhile. It is the sort of café that everyone wishes they had round the corner: busy, bright, airy, and where anything goes, from breakfast to candlelit evening meals.

"I think a lot of the **people** that live around here work from **home**, and so they often come in here for **informal** meetings, or just for a **break** so that they can get out of the **house**."
Isabela Hughes,
Joint Proprietor

"And we have lots of **mums** and kids. Younger **kids** and school children in the early evening – the mums bring them in for **hot chocolates** – and babies in the daytime. And **prenatal** classes go on and all sorts." Fiona Bell, Manager

It is a **great** place to work. The staff are great, people stay here a long time, **customers** come in for a long time and everybody knows everybody else. And that is one of the things I **like** about the place. I'm not from London and when I moved here I didn't find a sense of **community** until I came here. And that is what I like, a sense of belonging.
Fiona Bell

"It is a bit **different** from where I used to work. Before I came here I used to run a **Harvester**. I much prefer working at an independent place. When you come to work in the morning and you have to work out the **specials** it is really nice to be able to make up whatever you feel like. It is nice to have that **freedom**."

Dean Bradley, Second Chef

"I used to have a **favourite** table and I used to drive the staff **mad** if I couldn't sit there. But I am more **flexible** now." Kath Bilgora

"I used to go to the **Lyons** Coffee House in Muswell Hill and I'd always have a '**milk and a dash**'. Nowadays they call that a **caffe latte**." Carol Birdsall, Customer

"The **people** who come in here are mainly local, it is very much a local place. In fact, I think **Crouch End** is rather special, with all the little shops, it still has a **proper** little high street and you don't find that in many other areas of London anymore." **Isabela Hughes**

❝ You can just **sit** here and no one bothers you. And you can see **outside**, and you can't do that in many other cafés. **Carol Birdsall ❞**

"We're looking for a **chef**, so if the **book** doesn't take off you know where to come." Dean Bradley

"When you come out of your **shift** at five o'clock on a Saturday and you see the café **full** of people, and everyone looks **happy**, there is a certain sense of satisfaction. If I was working in an office, I'd go crazy." **Dean Bradley**

Chicken Caesar salad serves 4

Croûtons

4 thick slices of bread, cubed
60ml (2 fl oz) olive oil
1 garlic clove, crushed
1 teaspoon mixed herbs
25g (1oz) Parmesan cheese, grated

Dressing

40g (1½oz) Parmesan cheese, grated
1 egg
25g (1oz) tinned anchovies, chopped
1 dessertspoon capers
200ml (7 fl oz) olive oil
pepper

+

350g (12oz) cooked chicken breast, sliced
2 cos lettuces, roughly sliced

350g (12oz) Parmesan cheese, grated
sliced red pepper to garnish

Preheat the oven to 200C (400F/gas mark 6). To make the dressing, whisk together all the ingredients except the oil in an electric blender until well combined. With the motor still running, add the oil in a thin stream. The dressing will thicken as the oil is added. Season the dressing liberally with black pepper.

To make the croûtons, place the bread cubes in a mixing bowl and add all the other ingredients. Toss well to distribute the oil evenly, then tip the croûtons on to a baking sheet and spread out evenly. Place in the preheated oven and cook for about 15 minutes until golden, turning once or twice.

To assemble the salad, place the lettuce in a large bowl and toss with the dressing. Divide between the plates and top with the croûtons and sliced chicken. Sprinkle the grated Parmesan on top, then garnish with slices of red pepper and serve.

Lamb Cakes with Roasted Vegetables   serves 6

Lamb Cakes	Roasted Vegetables
1kg (2lb 4oz) minced lamb	½ aubergine, diced
grated zest of 2 lemons	1 small courgette, diced
2 egg whites	1 red pepper, diced
40g (1½oz) Parmesan, grated	½ onion, diced
1 tablespoon olive tapenade	a few mangetout
1 teaspoon pesto	4 baby corn, sliced
1 garlic clove, crushed	½ carrot, sliced
1 tablespoon mixed herbs	olive oil for drizzling
salt and pepper	

+

6 pitta breads

olives

tomato salsa

salad to garnish

> The head chef is **Ian Morrel**. And he is a **damn good** chef – although he doesn't like to **admit** it. Dean Bradley

Preheat the oven to 200C (400F/gas mark 6). Place the minced lamb in a bowl and add all the other ingredients for the lamb cakes. Mix well using your fingers, then refrigerate the mixture until you are ready to cook it. Place all the vegetables in a roasting tin or ovenproof dish and drizzle with olive oil. Season with salt and pepper and stir them around to make sure they are all lightly coated with oil. Place in the preheated oven and cook for about an hour until they are tender and lightly coloured.

With floured hands, form the lamb mixture into small patties and cook under a preheated hot grill or on a barbecue until nicely browned on the outside and just cooked inside.

Toast the pitta breads and arrange the lamb cakes on top of them to serve. Accompany with the roasted vegetables, a few olives, some salsa and a little salad to garnish.

Adams Café
77 Askew Road W12
020 8743 0572
Open: Mon–Fri, 7.30am–2.30pm, 7pm–11pm;
Sat, 8.30am–2pm, 7pm–11pm
Nearest tube: Shepherd's Bush/Ravenscourt Park
Bus route: 207, 266

The Blue Orange
65 Columbia Road E2
020 7366 9272
Open: Thurs–Fri, 10am–4pm; Sat, 9.30am–5pm;
Sun, 8am–4pm
Nearest tube/BR: Old Street/Liverpool Street/Bethnal Green

Café del Parc
167 Junction Road N19
020 7281 5684
Open: Wed–Fri, 7pm–10pm; Sat, 11.30am–4pm,
7pm–10pm; Sun 11.30am–4pm
Nearest tube: Tufnell Park
Bus route: 10, 134

Café Mozart
17 Swains Lane N6
020 8348 1384
Open: daily, 9am–10pm (last orders)
Nearest tube: Highgate
Nearest BR: Gospel Oak
Bus route: 214, C2, C11, C12

The Deli Bar
117 Charterhouse Street EC1
020 7253 2070
Open: Mon–Fri, 9am–11pm; Sat–Sun, by request
Nearest tube/BR: Barbican/Farringdon

Grace & Favour
35 North Cross Road SE22
020 8693 4400
Open: daily, 10am–6pm
Nearest BR: East Dulwich
Bus route: 40, 176, 185

The Green
60 New Kings Road SW6
020 7371 6763
Open: Mon–Fri, 7am–4pm; Sat–Sun, 8am–3pm
Nearest tube: Parson's Green

The Hive
Battersea Arts Centre, Lavender Hill SW11
020 7228 2286
Open: Mon, 10am–5pm; Tues–Sat, 10am–11pm;
Sun, 4pm–10pm
Nearest BR: Clapham Junction
Bus route: 35, 37, 77, 77a, 115, 319, 337, 345, C3, G1

Home Internet Café
1 Leicester Square WC2
020 7909 1111
Open: daily, 12 noon–8pm
Nearest tube: Leicester Square

Hubbub
269 Westferry Road E14
020 7987 0444
Open: Mon–Fri, 5pm–11pm; Sat, 11am–11pm; Sun,
11am–10.30pm
Nearest DLR: Mudchute

Jus Cafe
30–32 Fouberts Place W1
020 7734 7522
Open: Mon–Wed, 8am–6pm; Thurs, 8am–8pm; Fri,
8am–6pm; Sat–Sun, 12 noon–7pm
Nearest tube: Oxford Circus

Lounge
88 Atlantic Road SW9
020 7733 5229
Open: Mon–Sat, 8am–10pm; Sun, 9.30am–10pm
Nearest tube: Brixton

The Orangery
Kensington Palace W8
020 7376 0239
Open: March–Oct daily, 10am–6pm; Nov–Feb daily,
10am–5pm
Nearest tube: Queensway

The Organic Café
25 Lonsdale Road NW6
020 7372 1232
Open: daily, 9.30am–4pm, 7pm–12 midnight
Nearest tube/BR: Queen's Park

The Quiet Revolution
49 Old Street EC1
020 7253 5556
Open: Mon–Fri, 8am–11pm; Sat, 10am–11pm;
Sun, 10am–4pm
Nearest tube/BR: Old Street

The Ritz
150 Piccadilly W1
020 7493 8181
Open: Mon–Sat, 8am–11pm; Sun 8am–10.30pm
Nearest tube: Green Park

St Paul's Café
1 St Paul's Road N1
020 7359 3322
Open: Tues–Sat, 10am–4pm
Nearest tube/BR: Canonbury/Highbury and Islington
Bus route: 30, 38, 56, 73, 277, 341

S&M Café
268 Portobello Road W10
020 8968 8898
Open: Tues–Sun, 11am–10pm
Nearest tube: Ladbroke Grove

The Star Café
22 Great Chapel Street W1
020 7437 8778
Open: Mon–Fri, 7am–4pm
Nearest tube: Tottenham Court Road

Tate Modern Café
Sumner Street SE1
Open: Sun–Thurs, 10am–6pm; Fri–Sat, 10am–10pm
Nearest tube/BR: Southwark/Blackfriars

Victory Café
26 South Molton Lane W1
020 7495 6860
Open: Mon–Fri, 10am–5.30pm
Nearest tube: Bond Street

The World Café
130 Crouch Hill N8
020 8340 5635
Open: Mon–Sat, 9.30am–11pm; Sun, 9.30am–10.30pm
Nearest tube: Finsbury Park
Bus route: W3, W7, 41, 91

Index